ENCOUNTERS
WITH
HEAVEN

STORIES OF
GOD'S
SURPRISING
PRESENCE

KARIN J.
GUNDERSON

outskirtspress

DENVER, COLORADO

Encounters with Heaven
Stories of God's Surprising Presence
All Rights Reserved.
Copyright © 2013 Karin J. Gunderson
v2.0

Outskirts Press, Inc.
http://www.outskirtspress.com

Paperback ISBN: 978-1-4787-0843-8
Hardback ISBN: 978-1-4787-0797-4

Outskirts Press and the "OP" logo are trademarks belonging to Outskirts Press, Inc.

PRINTED IN THE UNITED STATES OF AMERICA

Encounters with Heaven — Gift Book & Music CD by Karin Gunderson

Purchase the **"gift version"** of this book with a music CD by Karin. Available only through www.ChristianHarpMusic.com or www.KaringJourney.com

The gift version is a hardcover copy of <u>Encounters with Heaven</u> with a beautiful CD of Karin's harp and vocal music.

The perfect, meaningful gift for

- friends
- those facing terminal illness
- those who are afraid of death
- those who suffer from stress or anxiety
- those who are going through difficult times
- every memorial service
- the grieving
- widows and widowers
- church libraries
- pastors and Christian workers
- caregivers
- birthdays
- teenagers
- hospice, hospital and nursing home volunteers
- hospice units
- hospital waiting rooms
- nursing homes
- Stephen's Ministers and anyone in a caring ministry

"Karin, I am a psychologist. I lost my dear wife one year, nine months and six days ago. You did more for me in one hour than all my colleagues did in one year, nine months and six days. Thank you." Dr. T. R. Minneapolis, MN

Contents

Foreword and Acknowledgements

There are many harpists who use music to bring peace to hospice patients in their last moments of life. So why should I, the voice of one harpist, write a book? I strongly believe this book can help us, as a society, dispel the myth that death is something to be avoided and feared. Rather, it is an awesome experience of the presence of God and of those who have gone before us. This book shares the often miraculous stories that happen as people journey toward their heavenly home.

When I began recording these experiences, I had no idea I would eventually be writing a book, so I must apologize that I was not able to ask each person for permission to share their beautiful experiences. Of course most names have been changed—except for those who asked me to retain their names—so identities will remain anonymous. I think most would like to share their stories, because they found comfort when I shared similar stories with them. Interestingly, for every story I recorded, there were often 10, 20, 50 or 100 more patients who had very similar experiences, so these are not unusual occurrences; they are actually normal.

The experiences within this book show that God's love for each of us can bring indescribable peace now and in the afterlife. At the end of each chapter, I summarize what we can learn from those stories, how that knowledge can change our lives now, and ideas for applying these changes to our lives. Then I close each chapter with a short devotional thought and prayer.

I would be remiss if I didn't thank the people God provided to help me in "birthing" this book. It really was a birthing process that took me eleven years! I began writing these stories a few years into my hospice work, as I realized they were too incredible not to share. The process of writing this book has been difficult, as I have relived some of the grief associated with hospice work and personal loss. At the same time, these stories are so encouraging and miraculous that the writing has strengthened my faith even more. So first of all, thank you to all who shared their experiences and stories with me. You have given a gift that will bless and encourage many people.

Thank you to all who helped me organize and write *Encounters with Heaven*. Sharon Davis, an English teacher, helped me begin by sorting the stories into categories. Linda Gillis shared her expertise in writing short stories from her *Guideposts* experiences and spent many hours crafting my stories. Julie Luedtke, published fiction author and technical writer, brought new enthusiasm just when I needed it. She encouraged me to finish writing and helped me with the final editing process. Julie had attended one of our family's Heavenly Harp concerts, and told her daughter, "She should write a book of her stories!" Later the Lord brought her daughter Kari and me together, and as we shared our first meal, Kari told me her mother was a published writer, and that Julie would be excited to edit the book. We had to laugh when we discovered that we share the same birthday, February 11—just a little sign that God meant us to work as a team! Julie and I have spent many hours side-by-side editing together.

In church choir rehearsal one night, I was telling my friend, Nance Wabshaw, about the progress on my book, and learned that she had done editing work for Tyndale Publishing. She offered me invaluable insight into the publishing world, and said she would also be willing to offer some editorial comments, since books often go through the editing process multiple times. Her comments were insightful, honest and timely!

My beloved husband, Jerry, used his precious free time to read through the entire book one last time. Catching any sentence that was rather awkwardly worded, he is the one who made sure that each sentence is clear and easy to understand.

Finally, my best friends and family prayed me through the struggles and work involved in the process of writing this book, so *Encounters with Heaven* could become available to you and those God has placed in your life.

Encounters with Heaven is meant to take away the fear of death:

"O death, where is your victory? O death, where is your sting?"
I Corinthians 15:55

As you read **Encounters with Heaven**, my prayer is that you will see the journey to heaven in a new light—that it is a beautiful homecoming to a gracious Savior, accompanied by loved ones, angels and miracles.

Thank you to all who helped me and prayed for me. You are precious to me. Thank you, God, for giving me a meaningful ministry that has made a real difference in the lives of hospice patients and their families, and that will continue to make a difference in the lives of all those who hear their stories.

And thank you most of all to my dear Lord Jesus, the One who makes it possible for *all* of us to say, "Death, where is your victory? O death, where is your sting?"

Chapter One
Karin's Personal Story

You may wonder how a Pastor's daughter who grew up in Billings, Montana became a harpist, let alone one who plays for hospice patients. The answer goes beyond playing the harp. I believe that God prepared me to become a harpist and a singer for the dying and their loved ones because of my personal losses, grief and experiences that mirror the hardships of those approaching death.

My parents loved music and singing, and it was part of my life for as long as I can remember. Whenever we traveled by car in Montana, the only available radio stations played country western music which my father didn't enjoy. Instead of listening to the radio, we would sing.

By the time I was six, Dad would take my sister and me along to sing for the patients in nursing homes when it was his turn to preside at monthly Communion services.

I was eight years old when my parents adopted my four-month-old baby brother, Paul. As Paul grew, he liked to pretend he was one of the current TV heroes, like "the Fonz" or Captain Marvel. Once when I was in seventh grade, my mom picked me up from a babysitter clinic with four-year-old Paul in tow. Paul leaped out of the car dressed in nothing but red tights and cowboy boots, with a bath towel fastened around his neck. He was there to save the day as Captain Marvel, despite the fact that I was mortified in front of my peers.

When my adolescence began, so did a ten-year period of personal loss of family members and close friends. As I worked through the grief from these losses, God became my strength.

During my junior high school years, I was part of group of girls who played in the band and hung out together. Cindy, Dena, Julie and I shared laughter, lunch and dreams for the future.

My first experience with grief and loss came when I was 13 and learned of Dena's death. Because her entire family had been killed in a plane crash, there was no memorial service and no opportunity for any kind of closure. This was the first seed God planted in my heart of the necessity of closure in the loss of friends and family.

Soon after this tragedy, life forced the harsh reality of grief on me yet again. When Paul was seven years old and I was 13, our dad was diagnosed with cancer of the larynx. I watched as my father, who to me was the epitome of strength and compassion, went through a regimen of radiation in order to survive. Dad was told he would never sing or speak again, but his faith never faltered throughout this ordeal, with prayers from people across the nation being extended on his behalf.

Although Dad's cancer subsided, he was still unable to speak or sing, so he would whistle along with the hymns on Sunday mornings in worship. As he continued to recover, our family experienced another devastating blow. Eight-year-old Paul was diagnosed with cancer of the brain stem that would prove terminal in less than half a year.

At one point, I watched Dad choke back his tears as Paul told him, "I guess I should trade in my bike for a wheelchair." As I watched my brother go through this deadly disease, I felt so powerless knowing that even as his big sister, I couldn't stop his pain or really help him in any way. When we learned he was dying, I wanted to do something special for him, so I saved my babysitting money and bought him a used electric guitar. Since I earned just fifty cents an hour, that $25.00 used guitar was the biggest, best thing I knew how to give him. He strummed it as he lay in his bed. Mom and Dad made sure he didn't use an amplifier often!

Toward the end of his life, about five months after his initial diagnosis, Paul was bed-ridden and no longer able to walk, eat or talk. The only way he could respond to our questions was to blink or move his eyes. One day Dad asked if he was scared and Paul's eyes raced wildly back and forth. He didn't understand what was happening to him. I wished so badly that I could take away that fear, but I had no personal experience with death. I felt helpless to comfort him.

I couldn't help my brother with his fears as he faced death, but God in his mercy went on to give me a ministry to help alleviate the fears of others facing death. Paul died soon after his ninth birthday. I was 16 years old.

At Paul's funeral, I slumped in my seat unable to do anything but sob. It seemed unbelievable to me that my dad could stand and sing with the powerful voice we never thought we would hear again. He used every bit of energy he possessed to belt out the hymns as if to say, "Death, you may have won the battle, but you've already LOST the war!" The Holy Spirit poured forth through him in power and might. His faith strengthened everyone present.

Following the funeral, I sensed the deep grief that persisted in my parents. In my sixteen-year-old mind, I feared my own grief would add to their intense pain, so I stopped grieving and buried my pain. I began to read the Bible and books like *Life after Death* and *Life after Life* to try to understand what happens when someone dies. Through the work of the Holy Spirit, I came to the certainty that this life is only a prelude to a much better life – a life with no more illness, grief or tears. I became sure that Jesus is the door to that life. He promised me that He'd be with me until the end of all time, so I could move forward, knowing that I would see Paul again in Heaven. Now my faith truly became my own. It continued to grow and helped me make it through each day.

Years later, I learned that grief is an ongoing process; a spiritual journey that continues to reveal itself long after the loss has taken place. We don't get over grief; we learn to integrate it into our lives. If we're fortunate we also learn to use our grief for good by caring for others in their grief.

The first time in my life I sang a solo at a funeral was for my high-school boyfriend's father. This was when I realized that singing was a gift the Lord had given me that could help others in their grief recovery. Around the time of that death, my grandfather's health began to deteriorate. I played and sang at his funeral as well.

After we graduated from high school in Billings, my best friend Cindy left for Washington to attend college, and I was off to Concordia College in Moorhead, Minnesota. There, I immersed myself in the music program. Singing soothed my soul.

A few months into college, I was shocked to learn Cindy had been struck and killed by a drunk driver while riding her bicycle. I couldn't believe she was dead too! Now only two of us remained from our junior high girls' group, and Julie had moved away before we graduated, so I knew she wouldn't be part of my life either. I sought solace in college friends and the Word of God. Devastated by Cindy's untimely death, I was comforted by the Lord in a very special way that I'll share later.

While at college, I met my future husband Jerry, also a music major. We shared much, including singing together in the Concordia Choir. After we married, we made our home in the Minneapolis area. Music continued to be central in our lives and work. We began thinking about having a family. Our journey to parenthood was marked with seemingly unending miscarriages, bringing more loss and grief into my already-battered life.

I would experience seven miscarriages in the next twelve years. Each one took a bit of my heart, but not my spirit. I was good at burying my grief, though my tears often streamed down as I wept openly in the shower each morning. We continued to try to have a child.

I vividly remember the first pregnancy; we celebrated the end of the first trimester by telling all our family and friends the good news! On Maundy Thursday, the night the Christian church celebrates the Last Supper before Jesus death on Good Friday, I started to bleed. Jerry and I went to the hospital that afternoon. The doctors found no heartbeat for the baby. Miscarriage again was inevitable.

Jerry needed to be at church in order to direct the choir and play the organ for the Maundy Thursday service. All of my friends would also be there, singing in the choir. At 5:30 p.m. Jerry left me alone on a sterile emergency room examination table in the hospital. Jerry and the choir at church prayed for me. Surprisingly, although I was alone, I felt totally at peace. I truly felt held in love. Suddenly Jerry walked through the door. I couldn't believe it. "What are you doing here?" It seemed he had only been gone 10 or 15 minutes.

"The service is over. It's almost 9 o'clock," Jerry responded with confusion. I was shocked. God had lifted me out of time! I had been awake, but completely unaware of time as I was held in God's hand for three and a half hours. Although we mourned over this miscarriage, I felt like I had been the recipient of a miracle that Maundy Thursday. The power of prayer became more of a reality to me in dealing with loss.

One year later to the day, I brought our first child, Joy Kristine, to her first church service. Born just five days before, Maundy Thursday was not only the day of her first church service, but would later be the day of her first Communion as a six-year-old. The trauma that filled the year leading up to her birth taught me many lessons that increased my empathy for the terminally ill.

While pregnant with Joy, I was bedridden from 28 weeks into the pregnancy through her birth at 36 weeks. The medication I was given to stop contractions and premature labor was intravenous Mag Sulfate. This drug caused me to throw up violently for hours, followed by severe headaches, double vision, and temporary paralysis that made me unable to move or breathe on my own. Each time I had to re-enter the hospital to receive Mag Sulfate I would sob, dreading the horrible side effects that left me completely helpless and paralyzed.

As I look back, the effects of this medicine taught me lessons that have been invaluable in dealing with the dying. In desiring to carry this pregnancy to term, I realized what it is like to feel compelled to do what the doctors say even though it will have unavoidable negative side effects. I know what it was like to be immobilized, paralyzed—unable to move from the neck down. I understand how hopeless it must feel to know you will never get out of bed again.

Not being able to breathe is extraordinarily scary, and helped me understand the experiences of those going through COPD, asthma, mesothelioma, emphysema, and ALS. The excruciating headaches and double vision reinforced the feeling of powerlessness as one is subject to the effects of medications or terminal illness. I realized how precious it is when a staff member crawls under your bed to retrieve your Chapstick, or assists you in something you can't do for yourself. This helped me to pay attention to things the dying might not be able to express, like needing a sip of water or a pillow adjustment.

Along with all these lessons, the miscarriages taught me about the difficulties of dealing with disabling pain and loss.

To this day, I recall a myriad of feelings from this difficult experience, but realize God has used each one for good. And out of all the agonizing experiences came pure Joy! I knew her name was to be Joy from the moment I learned about the pregnancy, before any ultrasound showed she was female. I knew she was God's gift to us, and she continues to be.

Shortly after Joy turned two years old, the Lord called Jerry to a new church music position in Phoenix, Arizona. With so many beloved friends and family in Minnesota, it proved difficult to leave. Throughout the miscarriages I'd experienced, we'd felt so much love and support. Yet we knew God was calling as all the circumstances fell into place perfectly, including three offers on the house we needed to sell. Now, we'd be alone in the Southwest. Three days before we were to fly to Phoenix, I miscarried again. I was devastated.

As we settled in and tried to deal with the loss of another child on top of the loss of our entire support network, I told my husband, Jerry, "I don't know why, but I just think I would feel better if I could play a harp." Since I was young I had been fascinated by the harp, but had assumed I would never have the means to acquire one. I admired the instrument's beauty and felt a connection to it. At this point in my life, as a music teacher married to a church music director, I again felt like the harp wasn't something that we could afford.

Although we had little extra income, Jerry was sensitive to the depth of my grief and agreed we would try to find a harp to soothe me. We scraped together money to rent a folk harp for a few months. I would practice gentle, sweet music as Joy lay down for her nap each day. Soon I felt we could not justify the ongoing expense and sadly brought it back to its owner.

A few years later, I was pregnant again. This pregnancy was identical to what I'd experienced while carrying Joy. I endured hospital trips, the Mag Sulfate, and all of its terrible side effects. But at 34-1/2 weeks our family welcomed a healthy baby boy, Ryan. After Ryan was born, one smile from him made it all seem worth the strife. Now, our family was complete.

At seven years of age, Joy's interest in learning to play the harp continued and became more persistent. She thought it was the most beautiful instrument and the only one for her. Jerry and I told her that if she got good at playing the piano, we would find a way to get a harp again. That year she covered in piano lessons what it took most of my students four or five years to accomplish. At Christmas, someone from our church gave us an anonymous gift of $2000, which has never happened before or since, so we knew it was a gift from God toward the purchase of a harp. I began taking lessons again, along with Joy. One and a half years later, I entered my first hospice home as a harp practitioner. Before this time I hadn't known what a hospice *unit* was, but learned that it was a critical care facility where terminally ill patients come to get their symptoms under control and then are released back to their homes. I appreciated that hospice focused on the patient's comfort rather than a cure, remembering that my brother was always so afraid to be left at the hospital with all the machines. I also remember how awful it was to say goodbye to Jerry for the night when I was in the hospital on bed rest, never knowing what terrifying side-effect would show up next from the medications I was forced to take.

As a result of the accumulation of experiences throughout my life, God led me to playing the harp and singing for hospice patients. God has used my past to bring me to the point of being an instrument of peace to suffering patients and their grieving families.

It gives me joy to sing and play the harp, helping patients go to their final resting place without anxiety, in complete calmness and peacefulness. In my hospice ministry, I can also assist families in realizing that their loved one's transition is a natural and inevitable part of life.

I believe that my personal losses have given me empathy with grieving families and terminal patients. God, in His graciousness, has given me a way to help others like I wished I could have helped my brother, but couldn't when I was only sixteen. He has allowed me to help others overcome the fear and intimidation of terminal illness and death through soothing music and stories like the ones you are about to read. I believe God provided Divine intervention in what could have been a crippling experience in my life—the death of my nine-year-old brother - for many reasons:

- So I would always notice Divine intervention in my life
- So I would appreciate and treat each day as a precious gift
- So I would appreciate my loved ones
- So I would realize my need for God in my life
- So I would learn to rest in God's loving arms
- So I could bless others as I longed to bless my brother
- So I would be a better "minister" to others—more caring, compassionate and sensitive to their needs

Looking back, the Lord obviously guided my journey toward the Ministry of Heavenly Harp.

My first wedding performance contained a spark of Divine intervention *and* a peek at God's sense of humor. It was a cold, damp, overcast February day with a blustery wind that gusted up to thirty miles per hour, an unusual event in Phoenix, Arizona. There was enough wind to blow over all the wedding bouquets next to the pond near the ninth hole of the posh golf course. The bridesmaids milled around in their spaghetti-strap dresses and goose bumps as the pre-service photo session drew to a close.

It was my first wedding as "the harpist." My fingers were aching with cold and I felt incredibly nervous. "What if I goof up the processional?" I thought, "I could ruin the whole wedding!"

Ten minutes before I was to play, I went to help pick up the bouquets and try to make them look presentable again. "Great," I thought as I returned to my harp, "Now my fingers are cold and wet!"

As I began the prelude, I put my stiff fingers to work and tentatively started playing. My harp was going out of tune so quickly that my husband stood next to me and re-tuned it as I played! Though I prayed, I just couldn't seem to get past my fear of the prospect of ruining this wedding if I played wrong notes or just generally "fell apart" in my harp playing.

Suddenly, out of the corner of my eye, I saw them approaching. It was an entire flock of ducks, waddling out of the pond, quacking softly and contentedly as they encircled me and my harp.

"I'm calling the ducks!" I giggled to my husband. A smile burst forth from the clouds of my fear and my anxiety vanished. Leave it to the Lord to use my favorite humor—slapstick—to break my tension and put a smile back on my face.

The wedding proceeded without any problems. Happily, the bride thought the music was beautiful, and I think the ducks liked it, too!

Chapter Two
Divine Intervention

This book shares the personal journeys of the dying as well as stories from their family and friends. The stories include the experiences of those who have been resuscitated from death and those who have been close enough to the end of this earthly journey to see through the veil between earth and heaven. Writing these stories has been a healing experience for me, helping me see the Divine at work in all areas of my life. The experiences within this book also show that God's love for each of us can bring about an indescribable peace now and in the afterlife. I hope you will find this for yourself as well.

The chapters of this book are organized in the order that most typically happens as people approach and go home to heaven. Often they experience Divine intervention in some form that helps them be aware that God is with them. Many experience Divine preparation that aids them in coming to peace with the reality of their mortality. As they draw closer to death they tend to experience the heavenly realm as part of everyday life. Finally, the Savior comes at the point of death for many people of all religions. After death, if something has been left unfinished, God in mercy often allows the departed to visit or show their presence and assure loved ones that all is well. It is my prayer you may find this information helpful when a loved one is facing mortality.

Through my work as a hospice harpist at the bedsides of hundreds as they journeyed home to heaven, I have come to know with certainty that:

1. No one dies alone.
2. We are loved by a God who cares about our personal needs and nothing we do or don't do changes that.
3. It is God's plan that we all act as one in love and support for each other.

4. At death, only the body is left behind, the soul is alive and freed from the limited version of consciousness that our physical body and brain endure in this life.
5. Those who have gone before us continue life in the spiritual realm. They often glorify God by continuing to minister to us as part of the *"great cloud of witnesses surrounding us." (Hebrews 12:1)*

Through my work as a harp practitioner in hospice critical care units, I have been given a taste of the beauty of what is to come. As God has made me a blessing to those in need, I have been blessed as well.

"All things work together for good for those who love God, who are called according to his purpose." Romans 8:28

Heavenly Harp Beginnings

On the 15th day of Dawn's coma, her best friend of 30 years, Gretchen, sat next to her bed as I played. The staff didn't know why Dawn was still alive; she was supposed to have died over a week earlier. I played and sang some favorite hymns, including "You are Mine," and shared a couple stories of God's grace at the point of death. Suddenly Gretchen looked at me and said, "You are the reason she's still here! I was supposed to meet you."

Something leapt inside me and I knew she was right. I left the room and Dawn departed this world, as if on cue that her work was accomplished that very afternoon.

Two weeks later, Dawn's only brother, Ray, arrived in town and wanted to hear the song "You are Mine" that Gretchen had been raving about. Gretchen also asked if I would share a couple stories. Ray decided I needed to make a CD of some of the stories along with my harp music and singing. Out of his vision came the dream of a ministry called "Heavenly Harp."

This all happened shortly after I finished reading Bruce Wilkinson's book, "The Dream Giver." The book let me dare to dream big for the first time in my life. I always wished I could help people not be afraid of dying after seeing the fear in my nine-year-old brother's eyes as he approached death.

Things began to move quickly and soon we had a ministry name, website and our first recording: "Heavenly Harp," a two-CD set. The first CD contained stories of God's provision for people going through difficult times along with favorite hymns and peaceful instrumentals with flute and harp. The second CD included the music without the spoken word. Our hope was that after hearing the stories with music a few times, perhaps people would pass the story/song CD on to someone else who needed it, and keep the second CD of music for themselves.

Four years into my hospice career, the ministry of Heavenly Harp began, with the mission of making the beauty and healing power of harp music combined with scripture and prayer available to anyone, anywhere, anytime.

We started doing concert tours on our way to and from taking Joy to college in Minnesota, with as many as 92 concerts per summer.

Since then, the ministry and healing of Heavenly Harp continues to spread and expand in new healing directions with an additional ministry, Karing Journey™. This book is the culmination of my hospice ministry, a collection of many of the stories that came out of my life as well as my work in hospice. Although names and some personal details have been altered, the stories are true. My prayer is that this book will bring hope, healing, and encouragement, as well as a personal, caring touch from God to you.

Without the Lord's Divine intervention, I would have missed the joy of helping others heal on a larger scale, through both the ministries of Heavenly Harp™ and Karing Journey™. May you find God's Divine intervention in your life as you read this book.

"I know the plans I have for you;" says the Lord, "plans for good and not for evil, for a future and hope." Jeremiah 29:11

One More Game of Pool

From joining his grandsons in a game of pool to not even knowing who they were, Grandpa had been declining, and it was painful for Jerry to watch. In the last couple years of his life, Grandpa Walter had become increasingly deaf, adding to his isolation. Now in the nursing home, he was confined to bed and his family sensed his departure drawing near. Jerry came to visit and stopped next to the pool table in the adjoining room. He reminisced about the fun times with his grandpa while he hit some balls around.

Suddenly his bed-ridden Grandpa *walked* into the room with a grin on his face and greeted him by name! "Hi Jerry! Can I join you for a game of pool?"

To Jerry's surprise, his grandpa's deafness had disappeared and he could hear perfectly. Jerry had been given the gift of a final conversation and one last game of pool with Grandpa.

> *"They brought to Jesus a deaf man who had an impediment in his speech; and they begged him to lay his hand on him. He took him aside in private, away from the crowd, and put His fingers into his ears, and He spat and touched his tongue. Then looking up to heaven, He sighed and said to him, 'Ephphatha', that is, 'Be opened.' And immediately his ears were opened, his tongue was released, and he spoke plainly." Mark 7:32-35*

What's for Breakfast?

I knew by the way the nurses were tiptoeing through the halls and avoiding room 105 that something was happening. One of the nurses met me in the hall and asked me to play for the distraught family. In room 105 lay two women; Dottie, who suffered a stroke five days earlier and never awakened, and Maria, who spoke only Spanish, and slipped in and out of consciousness. The nurse told me before I entered that Dottie was "actively dying." She was totally unresponsive and hadn't eaten for five days. The family had met with the mortician earlier that morning to plan her funeral, so emotions were running high.

Thinking that my music might be the catalyst for Dottie's departure to heaven, I played beautiful, relaxing music, and then I decided to sing "Oh Lord You Know Me Completely" (Psalm 139) for its comforting message and combination of English and Spanish lyrics.

Dottie, who had never awakened from her stroke, was clearly visible to me since the head of her bed was at a 45-degree angle. As I sang, she began to stretch, then a smile of satisfaction and joy crossed her face and she opened her eyes!

She quickly scanned the room, saw her son in a chair near her feet, and asked cheerily, "Where am I?"

"In the hospital; you had a stroke," her son stumbled, almost in shock.

"What's for breakfast? Can I get something to eat? I'm hungry!" Dottie blurted out. "I'm ready to go home, whenever you can get me out of here." Her children were dumbfounded. No one ever expected her to wake again.

Maybe the vibrations of my harp disintegrated the blood clot in her brain; maybe my harp music and singing gave her the ability and stimulation to wake up; or maybe the Lord just did another one of those awesome things He often does while I'm playing. Whatever happened, her family, who earlier that morning sat grieving the loss of her love in their lives, received a joyful surprise of Divine intervention.

"O Lord my God, I cried to you for help, and you have healed me."
Psalm 30:2

Way of Escape

Although the nurses didn't think he would want music, I kept being drawn toward Jermaine's room. When I arrived, I had asked the nurses if there was anyone who would really enjoy or benefit from the harp. They suggested several people whom I played for, but I kept being drawn back to play for this tall, big-boned African-American man, Jermaine. I entered and asked if he would like me to bring in the harp. He beamed! "I saw it in the hall but I didn't know you came into individual rooms!"

I set the harp near his bed and asked what kind of music he would like. He suggested hymns. I began playing and singing "How Great Thou Art." Soon his arms were raised in praise and we were both singing together at the top of our lungs. The nurse peeked in the room, obviously incredulous that her patient was singing with arms raised in the air.

After I finished several hymns, I walked to his bedside and said, "God bless you, Jermaine." He looked up at me tenderly and took my hand, "Today I have been in so much pain I didn't think I could take anymore. But the Lord says He will not test you beyond your ability, but will provide a way of escape. I feel your music has been my way of escape today. Thank you."

He squeezed my hand and I replied, "Thank you for the privilege of being able to lift up my brother in Christ." Then I left the room thanking God for using me for His glory.

"No test has seized you except what is common to people. And God is faithful; He will not let you be tested beyond what you can bear. But when you are tempted, He will also provide a way out so that you can stand up under it."
1 Corinthians 10:13

Peaceful Goodbye

One morning as I drove to the hospice unit, I felt led to pray for something I'd never really thought to pray about before--that the Lord would lead me specifically to a room where I might be a witness, building up someone who was struggling in faith.

I didn't feel any specific guidance, so I started in room number one, where I played for three women. One was watching *The Price is Right*, one was being bathed and the other wasn't waking up anymore. (She probably got the most out of it). While I was playing in room one, the nurse came and asked if I would play in room two. The daughter of the dying woman in that room was distraught and having the hardest time the nurse had ever seen with the approaching death of a loved one.

I arrived at the door and introduced myself to the daughter, Debbie, who was thrilled that I would come and offer music to them. Unconscious and near death, her mother Marian no longer responded. She struggled loudly for each breath as her lungs filled with fluid.

As soon as I started playing, Debbie burst into tears. She said, "I'm not really crying because I'm sad. It's just so beautiful…" After a pause to collect herself, Debbie continued, "When my Dad died a few years ago, it was terrible! We were in a hospital and the nurse came in and demanded, 'Why are you still crying?!' His death was so difficult. It was *awful!* Now, here I sit in this pretty room, looking out through lacey white curtains at a beautiful rosebush blooming in a garden and there's a harpist playing!" she sobbed.

I asked her if I could sing "You are Mine" for her. When she heard the words of love for her mother and herself, she sobbed all the more, but with utter gratitude to God. We talked and I told her how well-prepared people become before God takes them home. I also shared that it seems Jesus comes for people of all religions. Enthralled, she said the conversation really helped her. "I have been struggling with my faith because of the difficulty of my Dad's death," she confessed.

"Would you like me to pray with you?" I asked. With her nod of approval, I prayed, "Thank you, Lord, for the blessing of a wonderful mother. I can see how special she will always be by Debbie's love for her. Please bring comfort to Marian and bring her peacefully home at the right time. Right now, Jesus, we ask that you please ease her breathing and help her to relax into your arms. Comfort Debbie and her sister. May they feel Your loving arms around them in the midst of their grief."

As I finished the prayer, Debbie's sister walked in. I began playing some peaceful music and Debbie's sister, Linda said to her mother, "I'm here, Mom." As the music progressed, Marian's breathing became quiet. As I played, I said, "Debbie, look at your mom. Her breathing is totally normal."

She said, "Do you think it's the music?" I replied, "No. I think it's the prayer!" As I continued to play, her Mom's breaths got farther and farther apart. When her Mom hadn't taken a breath for about a minute, I suggested Debbie should probably get the nurse.

She asked, "Do you think this is it?" I nodded.

The nurse looked at the sisters and quietly confirmed what I knew: "She's gone."

They couldn't believe it. "Are you sure she's really gone... just like that?" Debbie asked, unable to fathom the news. The nurse reaffirmed her diagnosis. Debbie continued with heartfelt warmth, "Oh, Linda, she waited for you to get here! It was so beautiful and so peaceful!" They sobbed together and talked to their Mom. Debbie said, "Mommy, I'm so happy you had such a beautiful way to go, and I'm so happy you won't suffer anymore. You are in a beautiful place with Jesus now."

I continued to play for a while, and finally, I stood and hugged each of them. Debbie said, "You were sent by God!"

I replied, "Yes, I was. I prayed I might help someone in trouble this morning, someone struggling with their faith. This was the only room the nurses asked me to visit. The Lord must love you a lot!"

"He couldn't have taken my Mom in a more beautiful way," she replied.

"I sought the Lord and he answered me; he delivered me from all my fears." Psalm 34:4

God's Schedule, Not Mine

Sometimes what appears to be a frustrating mess is just the way the Lord brings us to the right place at the right time. Normally I play my harp at the Sun City hospice unit on Wednesdays, but my friend Nikki called Tuesday night and asked if I could play for her friend's sister, Sarah, who lay unconscious and close to death at St. Joseph's Hospital. I called Nikki as I arrived at the hospital at 8 a.m. She said she'd be there with another friend at about 9 a.m. I started playing, saving the song "You Are Mine" for her friend to hear. Finally at about 9:50 when they still weren't there, I told Sarah's husband that I must leave in order to have time to play at Sun City before teaching music lessons at home in the afternoon. I sang "You are Mine" for him and two friends of Sarah who had come to visit. They cried and thanked me as I packed up.

It was too far to haul my harp, music stand, and music to the parking ramp, so I left my harp at the information desk near the front door and walked to get my car. Confused about which street I would be exiting onto, I asked the attendant as I drove out of the parking ramp and then made the 20-mile drive to Sun City. When I arrived, I opened the trunk and found I'd left my harp back at the hospital!

After driving back to get it, I didn't have enough time to return to Sun City before music lessons, so I decided I could either be upset or just plan to play in Sun City on Friday, and go indulge myself with a free massage that a local store was offering. My husband Jerry tried to find a bright side and said, "Perhaps someone will need you on Friday in Sun City."

Friday came and I returned to Sun City. In the first room, the patient lay gasping for each breath and sounded like he was drowning. He died peacefully as I played.

In the second room, Paula sat vigil by her unconscious husband, Bob, knowing this precious man in her life would soon be gone. I sensed her isolation and asked if she had family in the Phoenix area. She told me she and her husband had just moved here and that she didn't know anyone. To make matters worse, ever since they had moved to Sun City, her daughter who lives nearby tended to "bite her head off" every time Paula called.

I played and sang songs of hope and Jesus' love. While I was playing in Bob's room, the nurse came and informed me that the patient in the next room had just died. The family was requesting my presence and music in their room. As soon as I moved to that room, Paula came to the door and asked if I could excuse myself for a moment. I stepped out and she gave me the news that her husband had died shortly after my music had stopped.

I returned to Bob's room as soon as I was available. "I think you should know, Paula, that I usually play here on Wednesdays and through a series of 'flukes' I ended up here today. Normally I wouldn't have been here." After explaining my missing harp on Wednesday, I said "My husband wondered if someone might need me in Sun City today. I believe I am here for you."

Paula called me to play for Bob's memorial service a few days later. After the service she gave me an envelope with my name on it.

At home that evening, I read Paula's note:

"Dear Karin,

I want you to know that I felt God had deserted me. However, I asked for a sign that this wasn't so.

I feel that you were my answer from God, because of the manner in which you happened to make an unplanned visit to the hospice.

Just wanted you to know. . .

Paula"

Tears ran down my face as my heart filled with gratitude that God used me in such a special way. God be with you, Paula, and may you know from now on that the Lord will never leave you alone or abandon you!

"Surely I am with you always, to the very end of the age."
Matthew 28:20b

A Step Away From Peace

Sometimes the person who seems the least ready to die is just a step away from peace. I asked Amy if she would like some harp music. She was a 42-year-old hospice patient with cancer throughout her body. She said yes, so I brought in my three loads of "stuff" and got set up. As soon as I began to play, she started talking on the phone with her psychic about her spirit guides and options for her advanced disease. I continued to play, but soon she became preoccupied with a large drawer full of paperwork while continuing to talk on the phone with her psychic about her disease. I sensed Amy wasn't allowing the music to comfort her, so I sadly excused myself and left her room.

When I returned to the hospice house a week later, I knew I would not get to each room, so I deliberately decided to skip Amy's room since she hadn't allowed the music to help her find peace. But the Lord had a different idea. A few minutes later, a nurse came to me and said, "Amy wants you to play for her again." I couldn't believe it. I was shocked.

I secluded myself in an empty room to pray and seek guidance. "Lord," I said, "if you want me to play for Amy instead of someone else today, please use this time in her room somehow."

As happened the week before, Amy continued with her busy-ness. This time she talked on the phone to her massage therapist while I played relaxing harp music. Eventually her lunch came and she had to quit talking in order to eat. Relieved at the Lord's impeccable timing, I played a beautiful piece called "Dreams of Spring."

When I finished the song, Amy looked up at me and said, "It must be wonderful to bring such beauty and peace into people's lives."

I answered, "It *is* a privilege and an honor, and if people are close to death the music often allows them to relax and let go." Then because I'd had that prayer time with the Lord, I took it a step further. "And you know what the most amazing thing is?"

"What?" she asked, now totally engaged.

"Jesus always comes."

"You've got to be kidding!" she retorted.

"No, really!"

"How do you know?"

I told Amy about the God-incidences of other hospice patients I'd been privileged to witness—how they see angels, loved ones who have gone before them and how Jesus comes when it's time to go home. I told her stories of Jesus coming for people of all religions and no religion.

I shared with Amy that many patients are ministered to by angels, by deceased family members, or by Jesus himself before their deaths.

Amy smiled and said, "You have no idea how helpful this has been to me!"

I replied, "If it's okay with you, I have a song I'd like to sing for you,that I think might be helpful at this point." She agreed, and I sang "You are Mine."

"I will come to you in the silence.
I will lift you from all your fear.
In the shadows of the night, I will be your light.
Be still and know I am here.
Do not be afraid I am with you.
I have called you, Amy, by name.
Come and follow me. I will bring you home.
I love you and you are mine."

While singing the beautiful lyrics of God's love for her, I saw peace in Amy for the first time. She stopped eating and listened intently. As the song finished, her eyes were filled with tears and she said, "No wonder I saw so much light in you!"

We hugged and I told her that she'd never be alone, that the Lord would be with her all the way, and that she was precious to Him. I began to pack up my harp and music. As I took the first load out of the room, I silently praised God for His grace in allowing me to share His love with Amy in spite of my skepticism and my plan to skip her room. When I entered her room again for the rest of my things, Amy was sitting with her head bowed. As I approached her, she sat up tall, grinned at me and said excitedly, "I just feel like... Hallelujah! Let's go!"

Amy was young and therefore stronger than most hospice patients. I looked forward to the opportunity to play for her again. However, when I returned the following week, I learned that, two days after my last visit, Amy stood up to look at something and suddenly died. I was so grateful God brought me into her room a second time!

"Do not fear, for I have redeemed you; I have called you by name, you are Mine." Isaiah 43:1

You are Mine

Yesterday, my friend prayed the Lord would work powerfully through me. Today He did! When I arrived at the East Valley hospice unit, Don, the chaplain asked if I could try to convince Chuck to let me play for him. Unable to believe he had to die before he turned 60, Chuck's anger poured out on all our sweet hospice staff. The social worker showed great concern that Chuck might try suicide.

I prayed before I entered the room and to my delight and surprise, Chuck seemed excited to have me play for him. I began with "Premiere Gymnopedie," a somewhat melancholy piece, because I thought he might be feeling sad, even though it was coming out in anger and frustration.

Chuck said he liked classical music, so I asked if he'd like me to play "Claire de Lune." He perked up when I mentioned that. As soon as I started playing it, I began to feel I was supposed to sing "You are Mine" for Chuck. For the next five minutes an inner battle ensued as I played "Claire de Lune".

"But I don't know if he even has a religion. It might offend him," I reasoned with the Lord.

"Sing 'You are Mine.'"

"Are you sure, Lord? What if he doesn't like it?"

"You must sing 'You are Mine.'"

"What if it sets him off and he decides to get me in trouble?"

"Sing 'You are Mine.'"

"Maybe I'm just making both ends of this conversation up in my own mind."

"No, sing 'You are Mine' for Chuck."

I finished "Claire de Lune" and Chuck loved it. I asked if he'd ever had the feeling he was supposed to do something, but had argued with himself whether it was right or not. I told him I really felt I was supposed to sing him a song called "You are Mine" and asked him if that would be okay. He said, "Well, you're two for two, so go ahead."

I began the song and tears immediately filled Chuck's eyes. I continued to sing as healing, soothing tears flowed freely down his cheeks. Just what he really needed—to release all that trapped emotion.

I finished the song and sat quietly, allowing him time to compose himself. Finally I stood and went over to his bed.

He grinned at me and said, "You have just played my three favorite songs in the whole world!"

I couldn't believe it! He knew "You are Mine" and it was his favorite hymn! His wife sang it regularly in the choir at their Catholic church, and Chuck *knew* the Lord had prompted me to sing it for him. I believe, for the first time in his life, he began to realize that Jesus loved him very personally and very much. A beautiful smile lit up his face and he thanked me profusely. Peace exuded from him. He said, "Will you write down the names of the three songs you played, because I won't remember them? My wife is going to flip when she hears about this."

After writing them down, we talked about some of the exciting experiences hospice patients have with Jesus and angels when I play for them. While we were talking, Chuck's wife entered the room. He had me tell her the story of playing his three favorite songs and asked if I would play and sing "You are Mine" for his wife. She sat next to him on his bed and they held hands. As I played and sang, they wept together, keenly aware that Jesus cared about them personally and was speaking to them directly.

The evening nurses who came on that day were completely confused with the report of an angry, suicidal patient when they met Chuck, now gentle and peaceful.

The third time I played for Chuck, the death rattle wracked his body. He could hardly speak anymore, so I played "Claire de Lune" and other pieces he loved. After ending with "You are Mine", I gave him a hug and told him the Lord would be taking good care of him. He could hardly speak, so he pulled me close and whispered in my ear, "I love you," then kissed my cheek.

With tears in my eyes I responded, "I love you too, Chuck, and I'll see you on the other side."

"Sing sweetly," he replied.

"I'll do my best, and you make sure to direct me to the right people and the right songs!"

"I will be glad and rejoice in your love, for you saw my affliction and knew the anguish of my soul." Psalm 31:7

"You are my hiding place; you will protect me from trouble and surround me with songs of deliverance." Psalm32:7

Last Valentine

Valentine's Day sends emotions whirling when a spouse is dying. Since Judy lay close to death, the nurses sent me to her room when I arrived, because she had loved my music so much the week before. As I entered her room, her husband's eyes filled with tears. "Our good friends sent this Valentine's Day card to Judy. It has things they wanted to tell her in person. I had hoped to read it to her, but I can't get her to wake up anymore!" Ed sobbed.

I responded, "Well, last week the music was really stimulating for Judy. Let's see if that works." He agreed, so I sang her favorite, "Amazing Grace," strong and clear. Within the first minute, her eyes opened and she looked like the many people I have watched when they see angels. By the time I finished the song, Judy was alert. "Ed, Judy is awake now so you can read the letter and you might want to give her a valentine message from yourself as well, since it may be your last chance. I'll leave so you can have some time to do that, and when you're done I'll come back and play some relaxing music for her." Ed thanked me and gratefully set about reading this last letter to his beloved wife.

Later I returned and played love songs as Judy fell back into a deep sleep while Ed held her hand.

"And now these three remain: faith, hope, and love. But the greatest of these is love." I Corinthians 13:13

The Smile

Together since they were 15 years old and married a total of 58 years, Shelly sobbed uncontrollably when she realized her husband, Mike, had passed away. The nurses asked if I would try to calm the family while they made phone calls and funeral arrangements. Shelly didn't know how to move forward without Mike. She asked the Lord for a sign so she would be assured they would both be okay.

Most upsetting to her were the last four days of his life because he didn't even look like her husband. His jaw hung open and his breathing was raspy with periods of increasing apnea. It was excruciating for her to see him that way. After he died, just looking at Mike in the hospice bed made Shelly wail. She couldn't stand the look of him with his mouth wide open. "That is not my Mike! Get the nurse in here and see if she can get his mouth closed!"

The nurse tried to close his jaw but it just kept dropping open, so they were forced to give up. Shelly came over and sat on the other side of the room next to me.

Mike had been gone almost an hour when I finally sang "You are Mine" for the family. Peace filled the room as I sang Jesus' words of love with Shelly and Mike's names included. Suddenly Mike's daughter called her mother to Mike's bedside.

"He's smiling!" Shelly gasped. The family gathered around him, astonished that the lips of the man who had left for heaven over an hour earlier were suddenly closed completely and formed into an upturned crescent... a smile!

Shelly breathed a sigh of relief, "Well, I guess I got my sign! He obviously wants me to know he's happy in heaven. Seeing his smile reassures me that I will be able to smile again, too."

Afterward in the nurses' station, his nurse confirmed that Mike's mouth had hung open for at least four days and that she had been unable to close it when he died. Although I have seen instances like this several times, she had *never* seen anything like that happen before. She did not believe me when I reported he was unexpectedly smiling, but she's a believer now!

> *"Ask, and it will be given to you; search, and you will find; knock, and the door will be opened for you." Matthew 7:7*

Conclusions

What can we learn from these stories of Divine Intervention?

1. We are not alone on this journey through life.

    "But we have this treasure in clay jars, so that it may be made clear that this extraordinary power belongs to God and does not come from us. We are afflicted in every way, but not crushed; perplexed, but not driven to despair; persecuted, but not forsaken; struck down, but not destroyed; always carrying in the body the death of Jesus, so that the life of Jesus may also be made visible in our bodies."
    2 Corinthians 4:7-10

2. God never gives up on us. There is nothing we can do to make Him stop loving us.

    "With everlasting love I will have compassion on you," says the Lord, your Redeemer." Isaiah 54:8b

    "I have loved you with an everlasting love; therefore I have continued my faithfulness to you." Jeremiah 31:3

3. When we belong to God, the Holy Spirit intervenes in our lives for our highest good, giving us a wonderful future and hope either here or in heaven.

    "I know the plans I have for you;" says the Lord, "plans for good and not for evil, for a future and hope." Jeremiah 29:11

4. God's Divine intervention in our lives is not only for our *good*, but also to bring us *joy!*

    "You bestow on us blessings forever; you make us glad with the joy of your presence." Psalm 21:6

    "...and do not be grieved, for the joy of the Lord is your strength." Nehemiah 8:10b

5. God wants to work through us, so that we may be an extension of Divine love and intervention to the world.

    "In the same way, let your light shine before others, so that they may see your good works and give glory to your Father in heaven." Matthew 5:16

    "Very truly, I tell you, the one who believes in me will also do the works that I do and, in fact, will do greater works than these, because I am going to the Father." John 14:12

How can this knowledge change our lives now?

- Knowing we are God's children enables us to see that some of the uncomfortable circumstances in our life are lovingly allowed by God for teaching and growth, just as any parent who really cares for their child's welfare must allow them to experience the consequences of some of their actions and guide them as they grow.

- Knowing God never gives up on us gives us freedom to make mistakes since we are assured our shortcomings don't lessen God's love for us.

- Knowing God is Divinely intervening in our lives helps us be on the lookout for the amazing circumstances and beauty God places in our lives daily. As we notice these things we are filled with gratitude and joy that God so lovingly cares for us.

- Knowing we are not alone gives us courage to step out of our comfort zone and follow God's calling in our lives.

- Knowing that God has chosen us and equips us to be light to the world empowers us bring His light and life into the lives of others.

Ideas for Practical Application

1. Look for God to bring good from the toughest circumstances of your life. Remember to thank Him for these circumstances, even though you may not feel like it, because *"...all things work together for good for those who love God who are called according to His purpose."* *Romans 8:28*

2. When you make a mistake, remember that the Lord still loves you just as much. Take time to appreciate that Heavenly comfort.

    "He has said, 'I will never leave you nor forsake you." Hebrews 13:5b

3. When God is calling you to something new, dare to try it. Then watch for the ways in which the Holy Spirit intervenes to empower you in your calling.

    "I can do all things through Christ who strengthens me." *Philippians 4:13*

4. Look for God to Divinely intervene in your life, perhaps with a beautiful sunset, a kind word from a friend or a stranger, circumstances that appear more than coincidental, or in a myriad of other ways. God's creativity in your life is boundless. When you see evidence of Divine intervention, thank God for caring for you.

    "Give thanks in all circumstances; for this is the will of God in Christ Jesus for you." I Thessalonians: 5:18

5. Keep a journal or a page on your computer where you can easily note instances of Divine intervention in your life. Looking back on this at difficult times will encourage you in your journey.

Devotional Thought

We are blessed in so many ways, yet often we choose to focus on what is *wrong* in our lives, or on things that cause us stress, fear or anxiety. Many times we are not even aware of our *background thoughts*—which are often automatic negative thoughts. Let's choose to give thanks for several blessings each time we realize our mind has begun dwelling in an area that causes us stress, fear, anxiety, grief, shame or guilt.

"Rejoice in the Lord always; again I will say, Rejoice! Let your gentleness be known to everyone. The Lord is near. Do not worry about anything, but in everything by prayer and supplication with thanksgiving let your requests be made known to God. And the peace of God, which surpasses all understanding, will guard your hearts and your minds in Christ Jesus.

"Finally, beloved, whatever is true, whatever is honorable, whatever is just, whatever is pure, whatever is pleasing, whatever is commendable, if there is any excellence and if there is anything worthy of praise, think about these things. Keep on doing the things that you have learned and received and heard and seen in me, and the God of peace will be with you." Philippians 4:4-9

Prayer

Thank you, Lord, for Your mercy and grace. Thank you for Your promise that You are *always* with me. Thank you that there is *nothing* I can do that could ever make You stop loving me. Thank you for Divinely intervening in my life on a regular basis. I am so grateful that Your care extends to even my smallest concerns and worries, and that You have plans for good for my life. It makes my heart happy to know You desire me to live a joy-filled life.

Train my thoughts to gratitude. Help me see my life from Your perspective so that I am enabled to give You thanks even for the difficult challenges in my life. Enable me to step out of my comfort zone when I hear You calling me to Your work in the world. Thank you for choosing me, calling, equipping and empowering me to be Your light and love in the lives of those You place in my path. Amen.

Chapter Three
Divine Preparation

Divine Preparation for the journey into eternity happens in a number of ways. It is always such a blessing to me when I have the honor of making a positive difference in the lives of grieving families in the last days, hours or even minutes of the patients' lives.

As I minister in hospice, I always pray that the Lord will prepare my heart and mind to find the right songs, say the right words and bring the healing power of God with me into each room. I always ask that I may be Jesus' light to all who cross my path.

Do Not Be Afraid

I saw the guilt, sadness and remorse on the faces of his parents, who had just arrived at the hospice unit from their nearby home. The nurse's face looked like a plea for mercy when she asked if I would play for Adam who was very close to death. Brought into the unit the night before, he was not expected to live through the night, but now it was nearly noon. Only 48 years old, Adam had no religion listed. Often, when a younger man dies, he's lived pretty "fast and hard." The parents asked if there was a chaplain who could perform his memorial service. Since they lived in town, it seemed obvious to me they didn't have a church home, so I began by playing some non-religious music.

After I finished a couple pieces, tears ran down the faces of both parents. Adam's mom, Lois, was on her second or third Kleenex and his Dad, Ken, sniffled as he wiped his nose with a handkerchief. I told them that people often cling to life if they are not sure they will be accepted into heaven. "I have a song that is Jesus speaking his acceptance and love; it might be helpful to Adam. Would you like me to sing it?"

They agreed. So I began,

"I will come to you in the silence.
I will lift you from all your fear.
You will hear My voice; I claim you as My choice.
Be still and know that I am here.
Do not be afraid, I am with you, Adam.
I have called you by name.
Come and follow Me, I will bring you home.
I love you and you are Mine."

By now Ken had his face entirely covered in the handkerchief as his body heaved with silent sobs. Lois had taken yet another Kleenex. I continued:

"I am hope for all who are hopeless.
I am eyes for all who long to see
In the shadows of the night, I will be your light.
Come and rest in Me."

All the little hairs on my body stood on end. I've come to recognize this often signals the departure of the person's spirit, or the presence of angels or Jesus. I looked over at Adam as I sang the chorus.

"Do not be afraid I am with you.
I have called you, Adam, by name.
Come and follow Me. I will bring you home.
I love you and you are Mine."

I knew through all the tears they were unaware of Adam's state. "Ken and Lois… Adam isn't breathing. He went with Jesus while I was singing the second verse." A stifled sob came from beneath Ken's handkerchief and Lois cried inconsolably as I began the last verse.

"I am the word that leads all to freedom.
I am the peace.....the world cannot give.
I will call your name, embracing all your pain,
Stand strong now, walk and live.
Do not be afraid I am with you Ken and Lois.
I have called you each by name.
Come and follow Me. I will bring you home.
I love you and you are mine.
I love you Adam, Ken and Lois, you're all mine."

As the ringing of the final chord faded, I told the exhausted parents I would get the nurse. As I spoke to the nurse, the chaplain arrived and asked if I thought Adam's parents would like him to come to Adam's room. I invited him to follow me back to Adam's room. As I played some peaceful music, he asked if he could offer any assistance. Lois sighed, "I can't even think right now."

"Would you like him to pray with you?" I asked.

"Yes." Lois replied.

The chaplain had Ken and Lois sit together and laid hands on their shoulders as they slumped under crushing grief. Pastor Lee thanked God for the loving and good memories of their son and offered meaningful prayer as I continued to play softly in the background. As he left the room, he said he'd be available if they needed him.

They seemed to appreciate the comfort of company, so I continued playing as they cried. Ken looked so broken; I felt in my heart that he thought he had somehow failed his son. I walked over to Ken, placed my hand on his shoulder and said, "Adam couldn't have had a more peaceful and beautiful death. I am sure Jesus came and brought him home."

At this point I think the Holy Spirit spoke through me, "Ken, the Lord knows you did the best you could for Adam. Everyone has to make choices; sometimes they're good, sometimes not so good, but that's how we learn." I hugged Ken and Lois and assured them God would be with them. Then I left them to say their final goodbyes.

I was thankful to be God's presence in Adam's room as I sang Jesus' words of love. This Divine preparation brought relief to his parents and peace to Adam. The gift of assurance their son received through Jesus' words allowed him to relax into Jesus' love and let go into heaven.

"Jesus said, 'Those who are well have no need of a physician, but those who are sick." Matthew 9:12

Mom's Favorite Song

I had just finished my morning devotions when the thought struck me to dig out my Christmas music. Although it was only November 2nd, I dug through the file cabinet, pulled out a Christmas book, and drove to hospice. I played for a Nazarene family who asked for hymns and relaxing music. "Do you have any other request?" I asked the daughter, Ruth.

She responded, "Well, this is going to sound funny, but my Mom's favorite song is 'Carol of the Bells'."

"You've got to be kidding!" I grinned. "I was on my way out the door to come here, when the thought occurred to me that I should bring a book of Christmas music even though it's the beginning of November, so I *just happen* to have 'Carol of the Bells' with me for the first time since last Christmas."

When Ruth found out how I added that piece to my music bag on a "whim" that very morning, she burst into tears and realized how personally the Lord cared for her Mom and her family. I was the one who received Divine preparation for my work that second day of November.

"You show me the path of life. In Your presence there is fullness of joy; in Your right hand are pleasures for evermore." Psalm 16:11

Christmas Homecoming

Christmas Eve day—what a tough time to watch a loved one die! Todd tossed and turned with severe terminal restlessness –a condition that is a normal part of the dying process before a more comatose stage. At this point, patients seem to know they need to depart and will typically try to get out of their bed or out of their clothes as they subconsciously search for a way to leave this realm. Todd struggled as he gasped for each breath. The man who sat at his bedside, Christopher, was visibly upset by Todd's plight. I told him my harp and vocals would help calm Todd, and he accepted my offer. I asked Christopher if Todd had any favorite hymns, because the solo harp music wasn't really doing the trick, and often hymns bring more peace. Christopher couldn't think of any hymns, so I asked if it would be okay if I sang "You are Mine." He agreed, and as I sang, Todd's gasping slowed slightly.

Christopher's concern continued, so I went to the restless patient, Todd, took his hand and spoke to him. "You know the Lord *does* love you and His angels are with you and will be ministering to you. The Lord is going to make your breathing easier, so you can just relax. He'll be with you, Todd." Todd's breathing quieted. I asked Christopher if he would like me to pray with them. He said "Yes."

"Dear Lord, Thank you for Todd. Thank you for his life and for the people he has positively influenced. Thank you for your love for him and for caring for him now. Thank you that you are making his breathing easier and thank you for your angels that are ministering to him."

At this point, Todd opened his eyes for the first time in several days. Because I've seen the look many times, I told Christopher, "He sees the angels." I finished the prayer and Todd's breathing became totally normal. I began to take my things out of the room and the third time I came back Christopher asked, "Is this the look?"

"Yes." I answered softly and reverently.

I sat down next to Todd and began humming one quiet Christmas carol after another. As I hummed, his breaths got farther and farther apart until he peacefully went home with Jesus and his angels.

What an honor for me to be able to bring a message of Jesus' love and acceptance on such a special day.

> *"'I will not leave you orphaned; I am coming to you. In a little while the world will no longer see me, but you will see me; because I live, you also will live." John 14:8-9*

On Eagle's Wings

I thought they wanted Christmas music, since they heard me from the hall and requested my presence. "Do you have a favorite type of music? I have classical, Christmas, hymns, waltzes, songs from movies and musicals…"

"Do you have any Hebrew spirituals?" asked Benjamin.

"I'm not sure, but I *do* have Hebrew celebrative pieces."

Benjamin must have ascertained I was Christian by my offerings, and as I started playing one of the traditional Israeli songs, he commented, "These pieces were actually being played when Christ walked the earth."

"Wow! That's really cool," I replied, surprised by his remark. As I continued to play, tears ran down his cheeks. He and his wife clasped hands. Tears flowed from her eyes as well. Needing a chance to vent their grief, this time blessed them and me. I asked if I could sing a setting of Psalm 91, "On Eagles Wings." They agreed. The words wrapped them in God's love:

"You who dwell in the shelter of the Lord, who abide in His shadow for life, say to the Lord, 'My refuge; my God, in whom I trust.'

And He will raise you up on eagles' wings, bear you on the breath of dawn; make you to shine like the sun, and hold you in the palm of His hand.

For to His angels He's given a command to guard you in all of your ways. Upon their hands they will bear you up, lest you dash your foot against a stone.

And He will raise you up on eagles' wings, bear you on the breath of dawn; make you to shine like the sun, and hold you in the palm of His hand."

I told them of the Jewish woman I played for earlier in the day who was seeing heaven and had a big grin on her face the whole time I was in the room. They commented on what a wonderful ministry my work is.

"It's really a blessing and an honor for me to be able to do what I know I am supposed to be doing," I said. "God bless you and keep you and may you have an easy transition back to your home tomorrow," I said as I went on my way.

Still crying, his wife caught me in the hall. "You did more for him than I thought you could do," she commented. "We both really needed a good cry, as you can see since I'm still crying."

"Tears are an important part of healing," I responded. "It was really a privilege for me to play for both of you." With that we parted ways, but not hearts.

"You who live in the shelter of the Most High,
who abide in the shadow of the Almighty,
will say to the Lord, 'My refuge and my fortress;
my God, in whom I trust.
For he will command his angels concerning you
to guard you in all your ways.
On their hands they will bear you up,
so that you will not dash your foot against a stone.
You will tread on the lion and the adder,
the young lion and the serpent you will trample under foot.
Those who love me, I will deliver;
I will protect those who know my name.
When they call to me, I will answer them;
I will be with them in trouble,
I will rescue them and honor them.
With long life I will satisfy them,
And show them my salvation." Psalm 91

The Perfect Birthday Gift

Her room glittered with the most festive decorations I'd seen in one of our hospice units; it was filled with colorful helium balloons and happy birthday signs, as three grown daughters determined to celebrate their 55-year-old Mom's birthday one more time. They were so thrilled that I would play for their Mom, Sharon, on her birthday, even though she hadn't awakened for several days. We enjoyed a wonderful birthday celebration.

As our time together came to an end, we joined in singing "Happy Birthday" to Sharon. Then I left the room, and so did she! The three daughters thought their mother's beautiful, peaceful departure was the perfect birthday gift!

"Every good and perfect gift is from above, coming down from the Father of the heavenly lights who does not change like shifting shadows." James 1:17

No More Grief

No physical reason existed for her impending death, but I knew why she lay dying…

Laurene's husband had just left for the day, so she was feeling at ease in speaking of the spiritual matters she had been contemplating. She wept freely as I sang hymns, and then she began sharing with me about her sister's death ten years earlier. Her husband had not allowed her to cry or grieve this death. Forced to say goodbye to her best friend, she spoke of how devastating her sister's death was to her.

Making things even worse, her father died shortly after her sister. The Holy Spirit showed me that trying to internalize the feelings of loss of her beloved mentor Dad and her sister literally crushed Laurene's health, as her husband would not allow her to cry or speak of the loss in his presence. Laurene's impending death stemmed from not being allowed to grieve! She had the choice to stay in this stifled life with her husband, attempting to deny all her feelings, or to join her sister and her father. Her husband ignored spiritual matters, but as a Christian, Laurene's relationship with her Lord remained the only thing that sustained her. She'd never been baptized and asked if I thought she should be before she died.

"Yes, I think it will be helpful for you because then you can know, beyond a doubt, that you are officially adopted into the Lord's family." I also reminded her of Mark 16:16, "The one who believes and is baptized will be saved." She joyfully responded that she would speak to the chaplain and arrange for her baptism.

Even though the baptism was held on the spur of the moment at a time when Laurene's husband would not be there, God provided for a beautiful event, because our only harpist-chaplain "happened" to come to the hospice unit at just the right time and was able to play for the extraordinarily meaningful service. Laurene and the hospice staff all felt God's presence and providence that day.

The chaplain told me afterward that my time with Laurene had been very precious to her. She really appreciated our conversation and the chance to share her pain and questions with another believer.

Laurene died within a few days of her baptism, and now she will be forever free from grief.

> *"See, the home of God is among mortals.*
> *He will dwell with them; they will be His peoples,*
> *and God Himself will be with them;*
> *He will wipe every tear from their eyes.*
> *Death will be no more;*
> *mourning and crying and pain will be no more,*
> *for the first things have passed away." Revelation 21:23-4*

Jesus Loves Me

The terrified look on Sheri's face silently screamed, "Help me!" As she struggled for each breath, I knew she didn't want to be alone. The nurses told me that everyone in section A of the hospice unit seemed kind of sleepy on this overcast day, but no one appeared to be particularly close to death. Concerned with Sheri's condition, I asked the nurse if this was her normal pattern of breathing. She confirmed this was a big change, and ran to get some medicine to ease her breathing.

While the nurse was gone, I asked Sheri if she would like me to pray with her since she seemed so scared. She nodded *yes,* so I prayed.

"Thank you, Lord, for Your love for Sheri. Thank you that You promise You will never leave us, so we never have to be alone or afraid. Please enfold Sheri now in Your peace and ease her breathing. Give her Your breath of life, and at the right time, bring her joyfully home to be with You and those she loves who have gone before her. In Jesus' name we pray. Amen."

As we waited for the nurse to return, I stood by Sheri's side, holding her hand. I silently asked the Lord that His healing power would flow through my hands to her. I held my other hand above her lungs as I sang "Jesus Loves Me". The nurse came back, administered the medicine and sat down next to Sheri as I returned to my harp and sang "Spirit Song."

> *"O let the Son of God enfold you,*
> *With His Spirit and His love*
> *Let Him fill your heart and satisfy your soul.*
> *O let Him have the things that hold you*
> *And His Spirit, like a dove,*
> *Will descend upon your life and make you whole.*
> *Jesus, O Jesus, come and fill your Lambs.*
> *Jesus, O Jesus, come and fill your Lambs."*

When I finished, the nurse stood and said, "She's gone."

Concerned about how Sheri's daughter, Lynn, would react when she arrived, I decided to play for the other two women in the room so I could be there for Lynn. When Lynn received the news as she entered the building, she came directly to the room and sat quietly with her Mom while I continued playing. After about 10 minutes, I asked her if I could have a few minutes of her time.

I spoke softly to Lynne, telling her how God had led me to her Mom, and to reporting her condition to the nurse, which I rarely do. I said her Mom remained alert to the end, and had asked me to pray with her. I told Lynne, "I held your mom's hand and sang 'Jesus Loves Me' until the nurse returned with her medicine." I concluded by telling her that her mom slipped away very peacefully as I played a hymn.

"I'm so glad someone was with her," Lynne responded. "I don't think anyone was with my Dad when he died in the hospital. It will be a happy day for my Mom as she is reunited with her best friend, my Dad, who died 10 years ago."

"Do not fear, for I am with you,
Do not be afraid, for I am your God;
I will strengthen you, I will help you,
I will uphold you with my victorious right hand."
Isaiah 41:10

He Knows My Name

The victim of abusive, alcoholic parents, Rick was removed from his home by the county and adopted by his aunt and uncle at age 11. By the time Rick moved in with his cousin Angie's family, his life-experiences had hardened his heart. Angie's father, a pastor, and her mother, Grace, taught all of their children, including Rick, about the Lord. Rick was unable to respond to this love and continued to live a very lost life as an adult.

At 42 years of age, Rick suffered a brain aneurism. Grace, his adopted mother, immediately went to be by his side for the following month. Rick lay in a coma with his eyes open, responding positively as Grace read from the Bible and shared Jesus' love with him. Doctors strongly suggested that she continue to read and talk to Rick because they knew he could hear every word. Although his eyes followed Grace as she walked around the room, they followed no one else.

After nearly a month, the doctors told Grace that Rick's brain function had deteriorated to that of a child, and he was dying. Grace called her daughter, Angie, that night, deeply grieving Rick's unsettled state of mind before the aneurism. Over the phone, Grace and Angie prayed vehemently to the Lord on Rick's behalf.

That night as Grace slept, she received the gift of a vivid, affirming dream. In the dream, she walked down a long path, holding hands with a young Ricky dressed in a three-piece suit. Instead of calling her Grace as he usually had, in the dream he called her "Mom," her true place in his life. Grace saw a large white wall that blocked the path. She felt nervous, not knowing what to do, but young Ricky strode on confidently.

Grace anxiously but honestly said to young Ricky, "I don't know what to do."

Ricky replied, "Don't worry Mom, He knows my name."

As Grace awoke from her dream, she realized that Rick had to become like a child in order to enter the kingdom of heaven. She immediately called Angie even though it was 4:00 a.m. Grace shared her dream with Angie, and her revelation that the Lord had now made Rick ready to live with Him forever. She also told Angie that they needed to let go of Rick. After they released Rick into the Lord's care, he went to his heavenly home within a few hours.

> *"Jesus called a child, whom he put among them, and said, 'Truly I tell you, unless you change and become like children, you will never enter the kingdom of heaven." Matthew 18:2-3*

The Peach

Overworked and exhausted, Evelyn had no idea that God was planning to lead her to deliver a beautiful gift. She worked as a nurse at a hospital in Alaska, and often traveled up to ten days at a time training nurse practitioners. One week, Evelyn worked three straight days at the hospital due to a staff shortage, taking brief catnaps only when she could no longer function. By the end of the third day she felt almost sick with exhaustion and ready to collapse. Kathy, a co-worker and good friend, invited Evelyn to recuperate at her home the following day. "I'll make a picnic and we can relax at the beach." Evelyn thought this sounded wonderful and readily accepted her invitation.

The next morning Evelyn arrived at Kathy's house and found Kathy standing hip-deep in boxes of peaches. Kathy's husband, a truck driver, had surprised her with the fresh peaches on his way to deliver groceries to another destination. They needed to be canned that day, as dozens were close to spoiling.

Kathy apologized that she wouldn't have time to go to the beach, but encouraged Evelyn to take the picnic and enjoy the beach without her. Although Evelyn knew this would be okay, she could see Kathy's project was overwhelming and offered to help can the peaches. They worked side by side well into the evening. There were many brown, shriveled leaves among the peaches, but one peach in particular caught the attention of both women. It was a perfect peach—the only one in all the crates that still had a beautiful, shiny green leaf attached. They set it aside to eat later.

When they finished their work, Kathy packed a half-dozen peaches into a paper bag for her friend to take home. She put the one with the vibrant, shiny, green leaf on top. As Evelyn drove, she soon came to the familiar fork in the road. One way would take her home. The other led to the hospital where she worked. Evelyn felt an urge to go to the hospital. She'd spent so much time there the last few days and was so tired that she was puzzled as to why she felt the need to return to the hospital. But she trusted this message from the Spirit and knew that whatever she decided—going home or going to the hospital—would be okay.

Evelyn took the road to the hospital. "I decided to follow that inner nudge, but I was so exhausted I wasn't really aware of what I was doing. I just followed the leading."

When she arrived at 10:40 p.m., the hospital doors were locked for the night. She had to ring the bell to be let in. With her bag of peaches in hand, Evelyn walked down the corridor, through the fourth door on the right and shuffled to the foot of the patient's bed. Lorraine had arrived only hours before and lay close to death. The puzzled family watched as this stranger, Evelyn, gingerly took the lovely peach with the shiny green leaf from the bag and held it up in Lorraine's view. A gasp of disbelief accompanied awestruck looks on the family's faces. The faces quickly turned from amazement to fear.

One of the family members stammered, "What are you doing here?"

"I don't know," Evelyn responded in confusion.

Lorraine's daughter proceeded to piece the story together for Evelyn. "My mom's dying wish was to smell and feel a fresh peach one last time. Today my dad stayed by Mom's bedside while the rest of our family searched the entire Alaskan peninsula for a fresh peach to fulfill Mom's dying wish. We were so discouraged when we were forced to return to Mom's bedside empty-handed."

Overwhelmed at being a vessel of Divine intervention, Evelyn brought the peach to Lorraine. Though she was very weak, a look of contentment came over Lorraine's face, when she felt the fuzzy peach and inhaled its sweet scent. She could now continue on the journey to her heavenly home knowing God cared about her every desire and loved her so much He would provide for her every need. She lay assured through Divine preparation. An hour later, with her family by her side, and the soft, fuzzy peach resting against her cheek, Lorraine departed with Jesus.

"Are not two sparrows sold for a penny? Yet not one of them will fall to the ground unperceived by your Father. And even the hairs of your head are all counted. So do not be afraid; you are of more value than many sparrows." Matthew 10:29-31

Is It Sunday Yet?

"Some of what he said seemed lucid, other things didn't," Gina told me, referring to her dad's last days. "It was getting kind of irritating. He kept asking, every day, many times a day, 'Is it Sunday yet?' Later he'd repeat, 'You're riding in a white car. You're eating a sandwich. You're laughing. You're riding in a white car. You're eating a sandwich. You're laughing.' After that he'd return to normal conversation and seem oriented to the present.

"He died on a Sunday, and then I knew why he kept asking, 'Is it Sunday yet?' He was waiting to go. On Thursday, my husband Tony and I were running late as we drove to the viewing. I asked Tony to buy sandwiches for us at the local deli. He picked me up in our new white car—a car that my dad had never seen. As he drove, we tried to quickly eat our sandwiches. Suddenly my husband slammed on the brakes as a car pulled out in front of us. The mayo, mustard and other sandwich ingredients got all over my face. I started laughing, realizing how silly I must look. Unexpectedly it all came flooding back to me: 'You're riding in a white car. You're eating a sandwich. You're laughing.' Dad had seen this already and had been comforted that I would still laugh after his departure."

"He will yet fill your mouth with laughter, and your lips with shouts of joy." Job 8: 21

Conclusions

What can we learn from these stories of Divine Preparation?

1. God has promised to help us in our weakness, and the Holy Spirit intercedes on our behalf.

    "Likewise the Spirit helps us in our weakness; for we do not know how to pray as we ought, but that very Spirit intercedes with sighs too deep for words. And God, who searches the heart, knows the mind of the Spirit, because the Spirit intercedes for the saints according to the will of God." Romans 8:26

2. Nothing is allowed into our lives from which God cannot bring some good.

    "We know that all things work together for good for those who love God, who are called according to his purpose." Romans 8:27-28

3. It's never too late to allow Divine intervention to bring about change in your life (even at the moment of death).

    "Those who love me, I will deliver; I will protect those who know my name. When they call to me, I will answer them; I will be with them in trouble, I will rescue them and honor them. With long life I will satisfy them, and show them my salvation." Psalm 91: 14-16

4. God hears our prayers and loves to answer in the ways that bring our highest good.

"Ask, and it will be given to you; search, and you will find; knock, and the door will be opened for you. For everyone who asks receives, and everyone who searches finds, and for everyone who knocks, the door will be opened. Is there anyone among you who, if your child asks for bread, will give a stone? Or if the child asks for a fish, will give a snake? If you then, who are evil, know how to give good gifts to your children, how much more will your Father in heaven give good things to those who ask Him!" Matthew 7:7-11

5. God can bring joy out of grief, laughter out of tears, meaning from things that appear meaningless, praise out of despair.

"The spirit of the Lord God is upon me,
because the Lord has anointed me;
he has sent me to bring good news to the oppressed,
to bind up the broken-hearted,
to proclaim liberty to the captives,
and release to the prisoners;
to proclaim the year of the Lord's favor,
and the day of vengeance of our God;
to comfort all who mourn;
to provide for those who mourn in Zion—
to give them a garland instead of ashes,
the oil of gladness instead of mourning,
the mantle of praise instead of a faint spirit.
They will be called oaks of righteousness,
the planting of the Lord, to display his glory."
Isaiah 61:1-3

How can this knowledge change your life now?

1. When we are weak, we can rest in the loving care of God, knowing that the Holy Spirit takes all our needs to God *"in sighs too deep for words." Romans 8:26*

    When difficulties enter our lives, we can patiently wait in the knowledge that they will pass, for the Bible tells us *"love never ends...And now faith, hope, and love abide, these three; and the greatest of these is love." Romans 13:8, 13*

2. We can let go of fear and anxiety about death, knowing God loves us, protects us, delivers us and honors us.

    "Cast all your anxiety on Him, because He cares for you."
    1 Peter 5:7

3. We can trust that God hears and loves to answer our prayers in the way that brings our highest good.

    "If you then, who are evil, know how to give good gifts to your children, how much more will your Father in heaven give good things to those who ask Him!" Matthew 7:7-10

4. We can expect renewed joy if we turn our lives over to God's loving hands.

    "You have turned my mourning into dancing;" Psalm 30:11a

Ideas for Practical Application

1. Think back over your life. Make a list in your journal or on your computer of things the Lord has done to divinely prepare you for something that you were or are to accomplish in this life.

    It has been very encouraging for me to see that, through my past experiences, God made me ready to minister to hospice patients and their families in *every* type of health crisis and dying circumstance. I had never really taken time to consider this until I wrote **Encounters with Heaven**. Noticing how thoroughly God prepared me literally amazes me.

2. Try visualizing God relieving you of your burdens. When you're too weak or tired to pray, just picture yourself releasing all your concerns and cares into God's all-encompassing hands. See how lovingly and easily He lifts them from you and cares for each one. See God smile at you with reassurance.

3. Use visualization to see God granting you the outcome you desire from a challenging situation. Thank God that the outcome will be used for His glory and for your highest good.

4. Since it's never too late for change, if there is something in your life that needs to change, lay it before God now. Give it to your Savior and start anew.

    "And He who was seated on the throne said, 'Behold, I am making all things new." Revelation 21:5

5. Refuse to let evil or negativity have the upper hand in your life. You have the power of God available to you.

Devotional Thoughts

We cannot always choose our circumstances, but we always have a choice in how we interpret them and respond to them. Choose to let nothing oppress you, for your spirit is *free* in Christ. Choose to be comforted, knowing you will be reunited with loved ones who have gone before you. Take comfort in God's promise that He is making all things new. He even transforms our worst circumstances for His glory. Choose to fill your life with praise instead of allowing your spirit to become weak and faint. Choose to display God's glory in every aspect of your life through the help of the Holy Spirit. The same power that raised Jesus from the dead is available to you. Claim your power in Christ.

Prayer

> *"I pray that the eyes of your heart may be enlightened in order that you may know the hope to which He has called you, the riches of His glorious inheritance in His holy people, and His incomparably great power for us who believe. **That power is the same as the mighty power He exerted when He raised Christ from the dead** and seated Him at His right hand in the heavenly realms, far above all rule and authority, power and dominion, and every name that is invoked, not only in the present age, but also in the age to come." Ephesians 1:18-21*

Loving God, enable me to live in Your power, that You may be glorified by my life. Help me keep my circumstances in perspective as I travel through each day that You have so generously given me. Inspire me to take the time to look back over my life and see how You have Divinely prepared me to do loving ministry wherever I am. Let me be so overwhelmed by Your grace that I can't help but to share it with others.

Help me remember when I am tired, weak, stressed, overwhelmed, ashamed, anxious or sad, that You already took all these burdensome emotions to the cross for me. I don't need to carry them. Gently remind me to place these things in Your able hands and then release them.

In Jesus' name I pray, Amen.

Chapter Four
The Importance of Forgiveness

Forgiveness is very important in being spiritually ready for the life beyond this one. Often, people need to make amends and be willing to forgive before they find a peaceful release from this life.

Family Reunion

No one seemed particularly engaged with the dying man. In the room three women sat silently--one leaning back in her chair near the window, another by the sink, and the third near the door. One asked if I could play "Amazing Grace." As I began to sing and play, she moved her chair from the door until her knees touched the man's bed. She gently placed his hand in her palm. The young woman near the sink stood, walked forward and placed her hands lightly over the dying man's toes. Soon the hardest looking woman rose from her chair near the window, walked over to the man and ever-so-lightly placed her hand on his shoulder.

I noticed a nurse observing at the door, but didn't think much of it. With each passing song, their touch grew more tender, as the first interlaced her fingers with the unconscious man, the second rubbed his feet and the third softly massaged his shoulders. Peace now pervaded the room, which had once been full of tension and uneasiness. The women took turns whispering their encouragement and love into the dying man's ear.

I gave each woman a hug as I left the room, and they seemed genuinely grateful for our time together. As I brought my harp near the nurses' station, the nurse who had been observing at the door motioned for me to follow her into the back room. "Do you have any idea what you have just done?!" she asked emotionally.

Confused, I answered, "No."

"Your music reconciled that dying man to the three daughters he abandoned when they were under ten years old! He had never contacted them since that time, until we called them yesterday. They agreed to stand vigil in his room, but they just sat silently. Not one touched him, spoke to him or even acknowledged his relationship to them as their Dad, until your music softened their hearts. What a gift you gave that family; forgiveness and reconciliation."

Overwhelmed with gratitude for the way the Lord used me, my eyes filled with tears and I thanked the nurse for sharing their story with me.

Then I left the room to return to my work, asking God to continue to use me for His glory.

> *"To forgive is to set a prisoner free and discover the prisoner was you." Unknown*

> *"Put away from you all bitterness and wrath and anger and wrangling and slander, together with all malice, and be kind to one another, tender-hearted, forgiving one another, as God in Christ has forgiven you. Therefore be imitators of God, as beloved children, and live in love, as Christ loved us and gave Himself up for us, a fragrant offering and sacrifice to God." Ephesians 4:31-5:2*

The Art of Forgiveness

"Jesus came to me and that is why I am still here. I am supposed to share my story with as many people as I can before he calls me home," she said as she looked up at me from her bedridden position. After joining me in hymns and relaxing during my harp solos, I came to Dorothy's bed, and she asked me to give her a goodbye hug. I gladly embraced her.

"Will you tell me your story you are supposed to share?" I asked.

"Yes," she replied enthusiastically.

"I was supposed to die within 24 hours because some doctors made a mistake. I had a subdural hematoma and the doctors kept giving me Coumadin. I was dying. My feet were ice cold and I was so chilled that my whole body ached. I could feel death's coldness spreading up through my body. They put a heating pad on my feet and covered me with six to eight inches of blankets, but I wasn't warming up. Finally I prayed, 'I'm ready to go home if you want to take me Lord, but show me what I need to do to prepare myself before I die.'

Soon, a large white sheet unrolled in front of my eyes, with a message in large, black capital letters: 'You must forgive the men who did this to you.'

I thought about it for a little while; then said, 'Yes, Lord, I do forgive them.'

Dorothy continued her story, "Within 15-20 minutes I could feel the warmth coming back into my feet and then spreading up through my whole body! The nurse came in and checked my feet and yelled, 'Her feet are warm!'

Since that day, I have lived many months in a group home and now I'm here at hospice with an unrelated illness."

"What a wonderful reminder of our need to forgive in order to receive God's healing," I responded.

Dorothy said she believed this was to be her message to the world. The other interesting part of her story was that her son went to her doctor the following day to give the doctor the good news of his mother's recovery, contrary to the doctor's gloomy "forecast" of less than 24 hours to live. Dorothy's son thanked the doctor for saving his mother.

"I didn't save her," he replied. "I had done everything I could and she was not turning around. This was a miraculous event."

"We are afflicted in every way, but not crushed; perplexed, but not driven to despair; persecuted, but not forsaken; struck down, but not destroyed; always carrying in the body the death of Jesus, so that the life of Jesus may also be made visible in our bodies."
2 Corinthians 4: 8-10

Free at Last!

When Marilyn's husband, Allen, felt he could endure the despair no longer, he ended his own life. Despite Marilyn's servant heart, and all her love for her husband, Allen suffered for years with depression that medications didn't seem to help. The suicide was devastating for Marilyn. Her best friend, Joan, feared she would never recover.

Joan told me, "One day, during my prayer time, Allen suddenly appeared in the room, in a physical body! He asked if I would please give his wife, Marilyn, a message. Enthusiastically I said, 'Of course!' He asked me to tell his wife how very sorry he felt for all the pain and grief he had caused her. He also wanted to make sure that she understood that she carried no responsibility in the suicide and should not harbor any guilt. Then he asked if I would also tell her that he is now free from depression and stress. He is completely at peace and happy."

Taking your own life is not an unpardonable sin, although it is never God's perfect will for you. We are to love and care for our bodies.

"Or do you not know that your body is a temple of the Holy Spirit within you, which you have from God, and that you are not your own?" 1 Corinthians 6:19

God's perfect will is that the timing of our physical death is left in our Creator's hands. We are not God, so we often do not understand how living a life that seems unbearable or fruitless may yet glorify God.

Having a loved one commit suicide is one of the most painful human experiences imaginable. It is a grief that seems more personal than any other kind, and leaves us feeling a confusing mix of emotions like loss, sadness, anger, shock, guilt, betrayal, shame, relief, blame, despair, abandonment, and confusion.

Many people who are grieving after a suicide become obsessed with the need to understand the person's reasons for their action. Mold allergies, alone, can trigger feelings of being unable to continue with this life and are at the root of many suicides. Needing to explain the person's actions can become overwhelming for those left behind, but may not be possible in this lifetime. Because of this, there may be a huge sense of responsibility for the death.

Other people get angry and feel as though the deceased went about the suicide to get back at them for something. This tends to make it more difficult to forgive the person they feel didn't consider or care about their feelings. Thankfully, in 2 Corinthians 12:9 God promises Paul (and us), *"My grace is sufficient for you, for My power is made perfect in weakness. Therefore I will boast all the more gladly about my weaknesses, so that Christ's power may rest on me."*

Ten More Days

Robert received a cross from his mother as he left to fight in World War II. Along with her prayers, she felt the cross would protect him. Robert reached the rank of lieutenant, making him responsible for many people. One day his men were bombed and almost the entire company died, but Robert survived.

After the war, Robert felt guilty that he lived when so many friends lost their lives. Likely due to his guilt, he remained sickly throughout his life. When he became very ill, Jesus appeared to him and asked if he was ready to go. Robert said, "No."

Jesus asked, "How long do you want to stay?"

After a little thought, Robert replied, "Ten days."

"How will you use the ten days?"

"I have some people I need to ask for forgiveness, and I need to say my goodbyes." With that Robert awoke and regained enough strength to fulfill his mission. He followed his plan.

On the morning of the tenth day his mother offered to cook breakfast. She asked what he would like and he quietly requested, "Scrambled eggs, please." When she returned, Robert lay dead with a peaceful smile on his face. His mother was struck with the knowledge that finally, after all these years, Robert found the peace and true freedom he had searched for since World War II.

"Do not be anxious about anything, but in everything, by prayer and petition, with thanksgiving, present your requests to God. And the peace of God, which transcends all understanding, will guard your hearts and your minds as you trust in Christ Jesus." Philippians 4:6-7

"In my experience, willingness to forgive is an integral part of spiritual health and an important way to prepare for the life to come."
Karin Gunderson

Conclusions

What can we learn from these stories of forgiveness?

1. We are held by the power of evil until we forgive.

    "Be angry but do not sin; do not let the sun go down on your anger, giving the devil a foothold." Ephesians 4:26-27

2. Forgiveness brings release from our shortcomings as well as from the chains of negative emotions forged by unforgiveness.

    "For if you forgive others their trespasses, your heavenly Father will also forgive you;" Matthew 6:9-14

    "So if the Son makes you free, you will be free indeed." John 8:36

3. Forgiveness brings healing.

    "For which is easier, to say, 'Your sins are forgiven,' or to say, 'Stand up and walk?'" Matthew 9:5

4. Forgiveness brings peace, joy and fruitfulness, because this act frees the Holy Spirit to work in our lives.

    "The fruit of the Spirit is love, joy, peace, patience, kindness, generosity, faithfulness, gentleness, and self-control." Galatians 5:22

5. We can choose forgiveness at any moment. It is in forgiving that we receive peace, and in forgiving that we are enabled to receive forgiveness for our *own* shortcomings.

"And when you stand praying, if you hold anything against anyone, forgive him, so that your Father in heaven may forgive you your sins."
Mark 11:25

How can this knowledge change your life?

1. You can find freedom as your forgive. Forgiveness brings release.

    "It is for freedom Christ has set us free. Stand firm, therefore, and do not submit again to a yoke of slavery." Galatians 5:1

2. You can experience healing and share that healing love with others who need it. Physical, emotional and spiritual healing begins with forgiveness. Negative emotions are often at the root of illness. After asking forgiveness, Robert, in our story above, found release from the guilt he carried, and regained mental and emotional health.

    "So if anyone is in Christ, there is a new creation: everything old has passed away; see, everything has become new!" 2 Corinthians 5:17

3. When you are released, you can experience the joy of helping others find release.

    "And He said to them, 'Go into all the world and proclaim the Good News to everyone.'" Mark 16:15

4. Your life can be more peaceful, fruitful and happy if you regularly forgive. Forgiveness brings increased JOY!!

    "There is therefore now no condemnation for those who are in Christ Jesus. For the law of the Spirit of life in Christ Jesus has set you free from the law of sin and of death." Romans 8:1-2

    "Blessed are those whose iniquities are forgiven, and whose sins are covered;" Romans 4:7

    "May the God of hope fill you with all joy and peace in believing, so that you may abound in hope by the power of the Holy Spirit." Romans 15:13

5. When our lives show the fruits of the Spirit, we bless the entire world
    with God's love and draw others towards that perfect Love.

    *"....let your light shine before others, so that may see your good works
    and give glory to your Father in heaven." Matthew 5:16*

    *"As difficult as it seems, you can be sure of this: At the core of the
    heart, you have the power to move beyond the old issues that are still
    hindering your freedom. The hardest things—the ones that push you
    up against your limits—are the very things you need to address to
    make a quantum leap into a fresh inner and outer life."*
    Doc Childre and Howard Martin

Ideas for Practical Application

- Consider memorizing Philippians 4.13: *"I can do all things through Christ who strengthens me."*

  If there is a certain person you are having trouble forgiving, consider using the technique of the man who brought his child to Jesus for healing in Mark 9:23-24. He said, *" 'if you are able to do anything, have pity on us and help us.'*

  Jesus said to him, 'If you are able!—All things can be done for the one who believes.'

  Immediately the father of the child cried out, 'I believe; help my unbelief!'"

  When you feel anger and feel you cannot forgive in your own power, cry out to God, "I forgive; help my unforgiveness! I believe you will help me forgive; increase my faith in my ability to forgive!" Know that you are not alone.

- Take a little time to consider the following questions:
  - » Do I know someone with whom I should make amends, so that I won't have regrets later?
  - » Have I put childish ways behind me, so I can see things from another's point of view as well as my own?
  - » Have I learned to be compassionate and forgiving?
  - » Am I using these days on earth wisely, on things of eternal importance, like mercy and forgiveness?

- Take time not only to forgive others, but also yourself, for things you wish you would have said or done differently. Make sure you forgive God as well, because this is who we often blame, consciously or unconsciously.

Devotional Thoughts

> *"Be angry but do not sin; do not let the sun go down on your anger, and do not make room for the evil one." Ephesians 4:26-27*

An unforgiving spirit is angry. When we hold onto anger we harm ourselves and those around us. St. Paul knew this, and hoped he could save us from this toxic mindset that keeps the heart blocked and unable to truly be thankful and loving. Jesus said:

> *"You have heard that it was said to those of ancient times, 'You shall not murder'; and 'whoever murders shall be liable to judgment.' But I say to you that if you are angry with a brother or sister, you will be liable to judgment;" Luke 5:21-22*

Jesus phrases this so strongly because the emotion of anger is a twin to murder. Anger is an act of murder inwardly and outwardly to those around you. Among other things, it kills joy, love, hope, goodwill, and self-esteem. Forgiveness is of utmost importance in finding peace and happiness again in your life.

When coping with the loss of a loved one whom you need to forgive, pray about how you are feeling. Tell God if you don't have the strength to forgive. God wants to give you His strength to enable you to let go, to forgive and to move forward. It's not too late to forgive someone even if they are no longer living. God is not bound by time, and you will not be free until you forgive.

Prayer

As Jesus taught His disciples to pray, He showed them the importance of forgiving others and of asking for forgiveness.

> *"Pray then in this way:*
> *Our Father in heaven,*
> *hallowed be your name.*
> *Your kingdom come.*
> *Your will be done,*
> *on earth as it is in heaven.*
> *Give us this day our daily bread.*
> *And forgive us our sins,*
> *as we also have forgiven those who sin against us.*
> *And do not bring us to the time of trial,*
> *but rescue us from the evil one.*

Dear merciful and compassionate God,

Help me mature in my faith, becoming a sacrifice of love to You in thanks for the gift of eternity You have given me. Prepare me for a joyful face-to-face meeting with You someday. In the meantime, let me not live my life estranged from anyone with whom I need to make amends.

Give me the courage to do what is right, and give me Your strength to forgive those whom I cannot forgive in my own strength. I forgive; help my unforgiveness!

Unleash joy in the reconciliation, so my life may be a witness to Your power and love. Thank you for Your Holy Spirit, who empowers me to forgive. Thank you for Your patient love for me. Help me live in Your love. In Jesus precious name I pray, Amen.

Chapter Five
Seeing Loved Ones Who Have Gone Before Us

Before dying, almost everyone sees friends or loved ones who are sent to answer their questions and ease the transition between this life and the next. When dying people see those who have gone before them, they rarely share it with their family, let alone with others, because they don't want people to think they are "going crazy." However, family members commonly hear their dying loved ones conversing with people the rest of the family cannot see. Often the patient will reach up to grasp an unseen hand, but if a family member offers their hand, it will be pushed away by the patient, indicating they do not want their earthly hand. Most families assume the patient's medications are just causing hallucinations.

After playing for over 25,000 patients and their families in hospice settings, my experience brings me to a strikingly different conclusion: *When a soul is soon to be released from its dying body, it is as though the veil between this "dimension" and the next begins to dissipate.* The harp tends to facilitate this opening between earth and the heavenly realm, and patients often begin asking questions about heaven; questions that all of us may have:

- "Will I be alone?" (No)
- "Will I be okay?" (Yes)
- "Are there dogs in heaven?" (Many have said there are dogs and horses and cats in heaven! And, according to an eight-year-old patient in one of our units, there are also some animals we don't have here on earth!)

Many patients see people they know who have gone before them. These ancestors and loved ones are sent to answer the questions of the dying and help relieve any fear or anxiety they may be experiencing. I believe this is a gift from our merciful God, whose Word repeatedly assures us, more than anything else: *"Do not be afraid."* God doesn't want us to fear, and the Holy Spirit in wisdom knows that whenever we approach something new for the first time, it is intimidating. Imagine how comforting it is to see someone we know, love, and have missed, coming to answer our questions and give us information about our upcoming journey—the step from this life into the next. The Bible tells us in Hebrews 12:1 that "we are surrounded by a great cloud of witnesses." I believe that our hospice patients are indeed seeing their friends and loved ones.

As I share these stories with families and patients, they share their stories with me. Most families have at least one story of someone who experienced "the other side." Similar scenarios are played out, over and over again, in the experiences I have witnessed. I only write down the truly unique ones. You may read this book with assurance that for every story I share, there are often 10-50 similar stories told to me that I did not write down.

These "stories" are not just hallucinations.

Unexpected Visitors

The first time I realized a patient actually experienced something from an unseen realm, it affected me so greatly that I never again doubted these stories. That day, I played my harp in a room with two men in beds separated by a curtain.

Niko, a man from Chechnya, lay unconscious on the side of the room farthest from the door. Brought to the hospice unit through the help of neighbors who called 911, he arrived a day before his roommate, Tom. Niko didn't speak English, had no family in the U.S., and never regained consciousness before he died. Tom, his American roommate, still alert and oriented to this world, was aware a roommate lay unconscious on the other side of the curtain, yet knew nothing else about Niko.

While I played the harp, Tom's wife came up to me, leaned over and quietly told me, "I was sitting next to Tom, alone in here with him and his roommate when I noticed Tom gazing around the room. All of a sudden he turned to me and asked, *'What are all these Chechnyans doing in here?!'* I couldn't see anyone else, but he was seeing almost 30 people!"

I acknowledged her revelation by saying, "He must have been seeing the ancestors and friends of the man on the other side of the curtain; he is from Chechnya!"

The invisible Chechnyans obviously came to surround Niko in his last hours. These visitors could not have been hallucinations, because Tom had no way of knowing his roommate was from Chechnya.

When people who have had similar experiences hear Tom's story, they feel enormous relief. Knowing that this is a normal part of the dying process is of great comfort to them. So as Grandma nears death, reaches up and says, "Mom, I've missed you so much!" the family will understand.

They may join in and say, "Do you see Grandma?! Tell us about her. What is she saying? Is anyone else there?" If the family knows the heavenly visitors are real, they are free to participate in this heavenly experience with their loved one. They receive comfort, as she does, in her vision.

In general, people go to their heavenly home when they are ready.

Doctors and nurses are often in disbelief as a patient inexplicably clings to life, waiting to make final amends or see a loved one for the last time. At other times a patient doesn't appear particularly close to death, but when all goodbyes are completed, they quickly go. Often, these encounters with visitors from the other side are part of the preparation process.

In my work as a hospice harpist, I find that such stories reassure families that their loved ones are never alone. This takes the pressure off the family so they don't feel they must remain with their dying loved one every minute, knowing their loved one is always accompanied.

"God never promises to remove us from our struggles. He does promise, however, to change the way we look at them." Max Lucado

A Heavenly Body

Monica revealed that her brother, Victor, died several years prior to their mother's move to hospice. After Victor's funeral, the family celebrated his life with a bonfire at their home. Monica's five-year-old daughter, Cielo, insisted her Uncle Victor was watching them near the fire. Monica tried to look in the places Cielo saw Victor, but she didn't see any evidence of her brother.

Monica recalled, "After everyone left the bonfire, late into the night, I heard a knock at my back door. I was so confused. The back door of my house is never used. It is overgrown with weeds and blocked by junk that needs to go to the dump. Everyone avoids that entrance to my home. The stairs are old, wooden and unstable. When someone comes up those stairs I hear the creaking. There was *no* creaking. My dog, who barks whenever anyone comes near the house, was silent. I crept to the back door and looked out. No one was there. I *knew* I had heard a knock. I opened the door, but didn't see anyone. The next day as I spoke to my family members, I found that each had received the same surprising knock in the night."

"Certain this must be Victor; I questioned Cielo further the next day. Her eyes were so joyful as she enthusiastically shared the vision of her Uncle Victor by the bonfire. 'He was happy we were all together. He looked at each person in the circle and he smiled like he was remembering the fun times we had together.'"

Since Cielo was young and Monica wasn't sure she remembered what Uncle Victor looked like, Monica asked her how he appeared. Cielo described Uncle Victor with long, thick, black hair, tall, with a strong, muscular build. This was not the thin, dying Victor, who had lost all his hair due to illness, but a younger, renewed version of her brother. When shown a family photo Cielo picked young Uncle Victor out immediately as the man she had seen by the fire. She experienced the joy of being the first to see her uncle Victor with his heavenly body restored to perfect health and vibrancy.

"Listen, I will tell you a mystery! We will not all die, but we will all be changed, in a moment, in the twinkling of an eye, at the last trumpet. For the trumpet will sound, and the dead will be raised imperishable, and we will be changed. For this perishable body must put on imperishability, and this mortal body must put on immortality. When this When this perishable body puts on imperishability, and this mortal body puts on immortality, then the saying that is written will be fulfilled:

'Death has been swallowed up in victory. Where, O death, is your victory? Where, O death, is your sting'

"The sting of death is sin, and the power of sin is the law. But thanks be to God, who gives us the victory through our Lord Jesus Christ."
1 Corinthians 15:51-57

Surrounded by Loved Ones

Donna's mother Leona seemed almost ready to take her place alongside her deceased husband. One morning Leona confided to Donna, "I saw your dad."

Donna felt her father's presence in that instant, as the words left her mother's mouth; she even smelled his aftershave lotion. She sensed the comfort this brought her mother, and now Donna felt that comfort too.

Leona then whispered in Donna's ear, "I saw my mother, too." Leona's visions have sustained Donna during this difficult time of goodbyes. Donna has a sense of assurance that her mother is not alone and will be lovingly escorted to a better place.

"Therefore, since we are surrounded by so great a cloud of witnesses, let us also lay aside every weight and the sin that clings so closely, and let us run with perseverance the race that is set before us, looking to Jesus the pioneer and perfecter of our faith, who for the sake of the joy that was set before Him endured the cross, disregarding its shame, and has taken His seat at the right hand of the throne of God."
Hebrews 12:1-2

Foretaste of the Feast to Come

Margaret's daughter Elaine told me her mother was in the hospital and not doing very well. When Elaine returned to her mom's room after a lunch break, she noticed Margaret's face had become beautifully luminescent; her shining skin glowed and was smooth as silk. Margaret now looked many years younger and her wrinkles were gone.

Dying Margaret recounted to her daughter, Elaine, details about the meal she had just eaten with her brothers and sisters. Although they all had died in their later years, she saw them at the meal in top physical form, and around 25-35 years of age—the same age that Margaret now appeared to be. Margaret also shared that she'd been reunited with her husband who had departed nine years earlier. Elaine sensed the truth of her mother's words reflected in the youthful look and brightness of Margaret's appearance.

> *"And the angel said to me, 'Write this: Blessed are those who are invited to the marriage supper of the Lamb.' And he said to me, 'These are true words of God.'" Revelation 19:9a*

The Mysterious Scent

Angela grew up on a tiny island that lies between Italy and Spain. She was in her thirties when her mother died. Now in hospice at age 48, Angela suffers from Grand Mal seizures that cause her to stop breathing, and one sent her into cardiac arrest.

She recounted, "I could see myself down below. As I was floating above my body, my mother came to me and gently ran her fingers through my hair, like she did when I was a little girl. I could smell the exotic talcum powder she used to wear. I have never smelled anything like it anywhere other than on that island." I looked at my mother and said, 'I love you, Mummy.'

"She answered sweetly, 'I love you too, Angela.'

"I told my mother that I didn't want to go back. Mother answered, 'You need to return Angela. I don't have your room ready yet, but when I do, I'll come and get you at the right time.'"

"Then I awoke back in my body, in absolute confusion. The nurse asked, 'What is that beautiful smell?' The scent of my mother's talcum powder emanated in my presence, and stayed with me for several weeks despite regular showers. Everyone who came near me would ask, 'What is that beautiful scent?'"

"For we are the aroma of Christ among those who are being saved, and among those who are perishing; to the one a fragrance from death to death, to the other a fragrance from life to life."
2 Corinthians 2:15-16

"But thanks be to God, who in Christ always leads us in triumphal procession, and through us spreads in every place the fragrance that comes from knowing Him." 2 Corinthians 2:14

Surprise Reunion

About mid-afternoon, I arrived in the little town of Chamberlain, South Dakota, to prepare for a concert at a Lutheran church that night. The pastor met me at the door and asked since I was there early, if I would do a little 15- minute presentation for a community action group of developmentally-delayed citizens between 20 and 60 years old. He said they were wonderful people. Enthusiastically, the pastor listed the many special things they accomplished around town, like raising money for flowers and planting them along Chamberlain's Main Street. He seemed positive the members of the group had never seen a harp before, let alone heard one played. He warned me, though, that they might be a little rowdy! I told him I thought I could handle it, since I'd taught 65 seventh graders in a public school choir.

We headed downtown to the smoky backroom of a little café. The pastor was right; the Community Action Group was excited, but once we got them seated, they relaxed into the music and many had tears streaming down their faces. We invited them to the concert that evening. The pastor and I left to get a bite to eat before the concert.

As we waited for our supper, the pastor began telling me about one of the men in the group. David, a member of their congregation for over 30 years, has Down's syndrome. Beloved by everyone because he loves everyone, he always has a hug for all who come through the church door. Now David is confined to a wheelchair. The pastor told me that David, an amazing 60 years old, had been doing very well physically until the recent death of his best friend, Denny. His health is now fragile so he needs the assistance of the wheelchair for mobility.

When we returned to the church, we were happily surprised that most of the Community Action Group attended the concert. The group sat in the front two rows of the sanctuary and grinned at me through the entire concert.

About halfway through the concert, I looked out and saw David, in his wheelchair, next to the second row of pews in the center aisle, excitedly waving at me. I couldn't wave back since I was playing the harp and singing, so I just smiled and kept singing. David whispered something rather noisily to his caregiver. Soon he began bouncing up and down, waving wildly, with the biggest grin on his face, but I still couldn't return his wave since I was playing and singing. This time, as he whispered excitedly to his caregiver, she burst into tears. I wondered, *"What is going on?!"*

After the concert, David's caregiver came to speak with me. "I just have to tell you that David has really been having a hard time since his best friend Denny died a year ago. During your concert, all of a sudden he leaned over and said, "I see Denny!" Then he really started jumping up and down and said, "And I see my DAD, too!" David's dad had been dead for over 50 years, since David was eight years old.

Even though we don't always have eyes to see them, it is wonderful to know we are surrounded by a great cloud of witnesses who encourage us and cheer us on our journey. In this way they continue their life's purpose: to glorify God by serving the Lord and others. The love of God is truly amazing!

"You have put more joy in my heart than they have when their grain and wine abound." Psalm 4:7

No More Pain

Suzanne recalled a childhood event that left a lifelong impression on her. "In the days before antibiotics my uncle was in a terrible car accident. Almost every bone in his body was broken and the broken bones had ripped open vital organs. He was dying and the doctors knew they could not save him, so they didn't even bother to set any bones.

Our whole family stayed at his bedside awaiting his imminent death, when suddenly, he sat straight up in bed, raised his broken arms in the air and said with a joyous smile, 'Nana, oh Nana! I've missed you so much!' We were shocked that he could move with so many broken bones and apparently not feel any pain. After he reached for Nana, his body appeared to be gently lowered back onto the bed, and he was gone.

"He will wipe every tear from their eyes. Death will be no more; mourning and crying and pain will be no more, for the first things have passed away." Revelation 21:4

Dancing Together Again

On February 13th as I drove home from my day of hospice work, I felt that I needed to go to Emmy's house and play. Our church choir accompanist for over 10 years, Emmy took her place as an extra mom to us when we moved 2000 miles from all our friends and family to follow the Lord's call to our new church. Emmy's husband and father of her five children had died twelve years earlier. She occasionally sensed his presence after his death because the scent of his pipe smoke would suddenly fill the room.

Emmy valiantly fought cancer recurrences twice, but the third time, when they tried to give her chemo, she went into cardiac arrest and they decided she would live out her final days with hospice service. Propped in the corner of a comfortable couch in her family room, she couldn't speak much anymore, but she smiled when she saw me. My harp music must have regulated her body and enabled her to talk, and we enjoyed a precious conversation. She told me she felt my husband, Jerry, the music director, was a gem of the church. I told her how much it meant to me to have an extra mom when mine lived so far away.

After I played a few more pieces, Emmy's daughter took me aside and asked if the choir could come and sing for her Mom one last time. I responded, "Well, there won't be choir tomorrow night because it's Valentine's Day, but the choir will be at the church tonight since it is Ash Wednesday. I bet I could get a group to come over after the service." Her daughter told me she would have Emmy take a nap and then be awake later when the choir members arrived.

Following the church service, cars began filling Emmy's cul-de-sac. Seated on a chair in her living room, Emmy grinned as she kept her eyes steadily focused on one area of the ceiling. It was obvious to me she was seeing angels or loved ones. She allowed each of us to give her a hug and enjoyed our singing. The neighbors began to come as they heard the music. The pastor offered us all Communion. Emmy continuously smiled, her cheeks seemingly tireless, but never looked directly at us; she refused to take her gaze from the corner of the ceiling and those unseen to us.

When dying, most people appear yellow, gray, or brownish, but not Emmy. She continued to become brighter white as the evening wore on. We had the privilege of watching her begin to transform from physical being to a glowing spiritual body.

To end our special time together, we sang a lullaby that Emmy wrote for her baby granddaughter, but inserted Emmy's name, saying, "Oh, Emmy, it's time to say goodnight." It promised the angels would keep her. There was not a dry eye in the room. We finished with one of Emmy's favorite hymns, "Precious Lord, Take My Hand."

Emmy died peacefully in her sleep early the next morning. As the pastor told the story of Emmy's death to the saddened choir members, she comforted us by revealing that Emmy's deceased husband had visited Emmy the week before her death and informed her that he would be dancing with her on their anniversary, February 14th. She knew in advance that would be the day of her homecoming. When I miss Emmy, I like to think of her abandoning her old worn-out body and dancing into a beautiful eternity with her beloved husband and her Lord.

"You will keep in perfect peace those whose minds are stayed on you, because they trust in you." Isaiah 26:3

Conclusions

What can we learn from these stories of those who have seen departed loved ones?

1. We can know with certainty that whatever we must endure, we are never alone in your suffering.

    "For we do not have a high priest who is unable to sympathize with our weaknesses, but we have one who in every respect has been tested as we are, yet without sin. Let us therefore approach the throne of grace with boldness, so that we may receive mercy and find grace to help in time of need." Hebrews 4:15-16

2. Even when we leave this body behind, we will be accompanied on our journey to heaven and we will never be alone.

    "And remember, I am with you always, to the end of the age." Matthew 28:20

3. There is a higher power at work that is obviously compassionate and does not want us to be anxious or fearful.

    "...be content with what you have; for He has said, 'I will never leave you or forsake you.' So we can say with confidence, 'The Lord is my helper; I will not be afraid. What can anyone do to me?'" Hebrews 12:5b-6

How can this knowledge change your life?

1. You can find peace for your everyday life, knowing that Jesus went through suffering like you do, so He understands.

   "For we do not have a high priest who is unable to sympathize with our weaknesses, but we have one who has been tempted in every way, just as we are—yet without sin." Hebrews 4:15

2. You can rest in the knowledge that you never face anything alone.

   "I am with you and will watch over you wherever you go." Genesis 28:15a

   "The Lord Himself goes before you and will be with you; He will never leave you nor forsake you. Do not be afraid; do not be discouraged." Deuteronomy 31:8

3. You never need to fear.

   "...Your eyes saw my unformed body. All the days ordained for me were written in your book before one of them came to be." Psalm 139:16

4. You never need to be anxious. You will be accompanied by Jesus every day.

   "Don't worry about anything; instead, pray about everything. Tell God what you need and thank Him for all He has done." Philippians 4:6

Ideas for Practical Application

1. Spend a little time quietly in God's presence each day. Practicing peacefulness or "mindfulness" will help you be able to achieve it more easily at stressful times. By purposefully giving your stress, anxiety, fears and worries to God, you free yourself for more productive things.

2. If this is a stressful time in your life, as you go to sleep at night, try visualizing yourself easily sailing through everything you encounter in life and everything you need to do, with Jesus by your side.

3. Each day find a quiet place and picture ten of your loved ones or friends who are already in heaven, smiling and happy that you are doing so well. See them happy that you have accomplished your dreams, as though all your dreams were already reality. Hear each of them give you words of encouragement and praise.

4. Try going for a walk with a loved one who has gone before you. Talk to them like you used to and hear responses like they would have given you.

Devotional Thought

What a joy to know we are surrounded by a great cloud of witnesses, cheering us on as we strive to finish the tasks which the Lord has chosen especially for us in this lifetime.

"Therefore, since we are surrounded by so great a cloud of witnesses, let us throw aside every weight and the sin that clings so closely, and let us run with perseverance the race that is set before us, looking to Jesus the pioneer and perfecter of our faith, who for the sake of the joy that was set before Him endured the cross, disregarding its shame, and has taken His seat at the right hand of the throne of God. Consider Him who endured such hostility against Himself from sinners, so that you may not grow weary or lose heart." Hebrews 12: 1-3

Prayer

May you be filled with the knowledge of God's will through the Spirit's wisdom and understanding, so that you may live a life worthy of the Lord and please Him in every way: bearing fruit in every good work, growing in the knowledge of God, being strengthened with all power according to His glorious might so that you may have great endurance and patience, and give joyful thanks to the Father, who has enabled you to share in the inheritance of the saints in the kingdom of light.

Colossians 1:9-12 (paraphrased)

In Jesus name we pray. Amen

Chapter Six
Visions of Angels

I first became aware of the presence and activity of angels as a five year old. My neighbor, Becky, would push me on the 16-foot tall school swing set across the street from my house. I felt like I could fly and I loved it as she would send me higher and higher until the chain would jerk because the swing was even with the top of the swing set.

One day when the chain jerked I lost my grip and went flying up and out in an arch from the top of the swing set. It was a surreal event as it seemed to happen in slow motion. My arms went straight out from my sides so my body looked like a "t" and I was lowered to the ground by unseen angels. When I landed there was no jolt and instead of being thrown forward, I came straight down and landed softly on flat feet, as though my mom had lowered me to the ground.

Maybe that is why I wasn't so surprised when my neighbor shared her son's experience with me. Four-year-old Jonny often biked recklessly off the end of his family's driveway into the open road without the slightest thought that an approaching car could end his life. He was unattended much of the time as his mother fought depression and drug abuse, and I prayed for angels to guard him. I later befriended his mother, and she has remained a lifelong friend. She related this story of Jonny and his angels.

"Sitting on the front step of the house, I watched my 5-year-old son, Jonny, ride his new birthday bike—his first bike with handbrakes. He raced down the street, showing off how fast his new bike could go. Suddenly he jammed on the handbrakes. I watched in horror as his bike flipped forward on its front wheel and Jonny went into a handstand above the handlebars. The bike came back down, but Jonny's face continued flying directly toward the pavement.

"Every muscle in my body tensed and I flinched, horrified, fearing the worst. Then the most incredible thing happened. His body flipped over into a sitting position where he remained momentarily, and then his feet gently came down on the ground. He landed standing up! I sat stunned and motionless. Jonny abandoned his bike in the road and came running toward me, 'Did you see them? Did you see them?!'

"'What?' I asked, still in shock.

"'The angels set me down!'

"Beginning to recover my composure, I responded, 'I didn't see them, but I saw how softly you landed. It was unbelievable!'

"'The angels set me down!' he repeated triumphantly and skipped off to retrieve his bike and race down the road again."

"For He will command his angels concerning you to guard you in all your ways; they will lift you up in their hands, so that you will not strike your foot against a stone." Psalm 91:11

My First Day

On the day I began my hospice ministry, I entered the first patient's room with a little trepidation. I introduced myself to the woman's daughter, Ruth, and told her that hospice sends me from room to room to play for the patients because it makes them more comfortable. She invited me in. Immediately, I saw that Ruth was very agitated because she couldn't wake her mom anymore. As I played peaceful music, she kept shaking her mother and saying "Mom, wake up."

I decided to ask Ruth if her mom had a favorite hymn, hoping a hymn would soothe Ruth. She said her mom loved "Amazing Grace," so I began to sing and play it. Ruth kept trying to wake her mother, but by the second verse she settled down quietly in a seat at the bedside and gazed at her mom. Suddenly, during the last verse, as I sang "When we've been there 10,000 years, bright shining as the sun...," Ruth's mom opened her eyes. Ruth jumped up and leaned over her mother and whispered, "I love you, Mom." Her mother closed her eyes again after about 20 seconds.

Ruth later called and asked if I would play for the funeral; her mom had died very peacefully a few minutes after I left her room. Ruth confided, "Mom opened her eyes but she wasn't looking at me. I'm sure she saw angels. I really feel like your song opened the door for the angels to come into the room. That's why it's so important to me to have you play for her memorial service."

Since that first day, it has become so common for me to see people looking at angels that I know "the look" immediately. Usually they aren't peering at a bright spot in the room, or toward a window, but toward a dark, upper corner of the ceiling. Their eyes grow large, and even if I put my face right in their line of sight a few inches from them, they look right through me with this ecstatic or awestruck look that cannot be shaken.

Often the patient's eyes appear to be following movement above them, which I have come to realize is dancing angels. What is most meaningful to me is how often the patients tell me the angels are hovering right behind me or above me.

"Are not all angels ministering spirits sent to serve those who will inherit salvation?" Hebrews 1:14

"Do Your Thing, Sue"

A thin, teetering, withered old woman, Sue, joined our church choir, but I soon realized she was no ordinary woman. She sang in the soprano section; the only problem—everything she sang came out an octave lower than written. I quickly learned to appreciate Sue, who blessed many people in her career as a nurse. "I nursed my husband through nearly ten years of Alzheimer's," she told me. "After he died, I was alone for several years. Then the Lord blessed me by bringing another man into my life; he was my true soul-mate. I loved him so much! We decided to go on a cruise after we got married. One afternoon, we went back to our cabin for a rest before the evening's festivities. He fell asleep quickly, and I just laid there on my back thinking about what a gift he was to me.

"Suddenly, I saw a ladder coming down through the ceiling of the cabin with angels going up and down. A beautiful, dark-haired angel climbed off the ladder, came to my side of the bed, bent down, and gently kissed me on the lips. I was so surprised that I just lay completely still and didn't move. I wondered what this could mean. The angel smiled sweetly at me with a look of compassion, and then ascended the ladder and the ladder disappeared. Now I believe that compassionate look had to do with her foreknowledge that I would soon face another torturous time, watching another husband deteriorate and die of Alzheimer's disease. Something in that encounter instilled the power of God's healing within me. I think it was her kiss.

"I was a 'float' nurse and every day the Lord would put me on the hospital floor where He needed me. I didn't think anyone knew God had given me the gift of healing those I touched.

"One night I was working in the emergency room. A young man was admitted with a traumatic brain injury. He had been in a motorcycle accident without a helmet. The doctor did all he could, but the injuries were too extensive.

"The doctor shook his head sadly. You could see he was thinking, '*What a waste.*' He said to the staff 'There is nothing else I can do. He's not going to make it through the night.' Then he turned to me and said, 'Do your thing, Sue.' I couldn't believe he knew! So I did 'my thing.' I prayed and laid my hands on the motorcyclist's broken body and placed them near his broken skull.

"I didn't hear what happened to the man, but I was really surprised when I saw him out of Critical Care, and on the rehab floor of the hospital two weeks later! He was there a couple more weeks and then released to go home.

What a joy it has been to be able to bless people with the Lord's healing!"

"And he dreamed that there was a ladder set up on the earth, the top of it reaching to heaven; and the angels of God were ascending and descending on it." Genesis 28.12

Grandma's Guardian Angels

A lovely, faith-filled grandma, Agnes has a story that could make any-one a believer in angels! We were talking about how God prepares people before they die, and that angels often minister to them. Hearing that I believed in angels, she decided to share her angel experiences with me.

"My husband had been dead less than a year when I was declared legally blind. I was working on a sewing project that I really wanted to finish, so I decided to drive to the fabric store three blocks from my house to get what I needed. I used my right turn signal and began to change lanes when suddenly I realized I was less than an inch from a car in the next lane. I cried out, 'Jesus, help me!' Suddenly I was out of the situation, but I was so shaken that I pulled off to the side of the road.

A man who was walking a dog nearby poked his head in the window and asked, 'Are you okay?'

"I replied, 'Yes, I'm just a little shook up.'

"Then he asked, 'What happened to the two men who pushed your car out of the way?' There were no other men anywhere in sight!"

Agnes then shared another angel story. "I was crossing a street, and a car came careening around the corner and I knew it was going to hit me. I cried out to the Lord as I began to feel the car brush across my leg. Instantly, I was out of the crosswalk and sitting on a bus bench on the opposite side of the road. I had no idea how I'd gotten there. The man sitting next to me on the bench looked at me and said, 'What happened to the two men who saved your life?!' Once again, the "mystery men" were nowhere to be seen!

"See I am sending an angel ahead of you to guard you along the way."
Exodus 23:20

"The Other Things Come at Night"

I had no idea Clara had been involved in a cult. Playing some peaceful music for her and her roommate, I asked if they had any favorite hymns. I played a request from Anna, not realizing Clara had no Christian background. Next I played "You are Mine." The refrain says, *"Do not be afraid I am with you. I have called you each by name. Come and follow me. I will bring you home. I love you and you are mine."*

When I finished, I felt moved to go to Clara and tell her she was precious, she would not be alone, and she didn't need to be afraid. I told her that Jesus would come for her, but in the meantime His angels would minister to her. She responded fearfully, "But the other things come at night."

I said, "Well, that doesn't need to happen. Let's pray about it." She thought that sounded like a good idea, so we prayed. I asked the Lord to protect her from anything evil in the room or in her. I asked that she would be surrounded by His angels. We said, "Amen" together.

As she opened her eyes, she pointed to the blank wall directly behind me and asked, "Who's that?"

As I turned toward the wall I responded, "Well it's not a person, so it must be the angel the Lord sent to protect you! Wow! That was a fast answer to prayer! See how much He loves you! God is taking care of you so you don't have to be afraid!"

"You will not fear the terror of night," Psalm 91:5a

Angel Dance

Edna lay unresponsive while puzzled doctors maintained there was no reason she should still be alive. They thought there must be some reason she was still hanging on. For the last few years, Edna, a diminutive woman with soft, fine platinum hair, had lived with her granddaughter, Michelle, and Michelle's husband. As I played in Edna's room, Michelle expressed her grief and focused with fondness on Edna's life. Michelle remembered the previous spring when she organized an Easter egg hunt for Edna in their yard.

Michelle spoke of the beauty of Edna's hospice experience, which included an angel encounter. "It was just a few days ago," Michelle began, "I was sitting next to Grandma's bed and she was looking up at a television that wasn't turned on. She glanced toward me and revealed in a secretive whisper, 'There are angels here.'

"I thought I'd humor her and replied, 'They must be lovely.'

"'They are!' Edna exclaimed.

"'What do they look like?' I asked, now more interested in what would come next.

"'They are blue and silver!'

"'They must be beautiful,' I confirmed.

"'Yes! There are six of them.'

"'What are they doing?' I asked.

"Grandma looked at me in exasperation and rolled her eyes as though saying, *'Why don't you just look at them yourself?'*

"I couldn't see them, so Grandma exclaimed, 'They're dancing of course!'

"My Grandma absolutely loved to dance! It is so perfect that the angels who accompanied her were dancing!"

"Let them praise his name with dancing, making melody to him with tambourine and lyre." Psalm 149:3

Waving at the Angels

Coming out of a life of darkness and drug addiction, when Kathy found the Lord, she felt the need to cover her home in the protection of guardian angels. We went through her home and blessed each room with prayer, asking the Lord to fill her house with angels. Her four-year-old daughter, Faith, could see the angels occasionally.

Faith's dad, Scott, who never married her mother, occasionally visited Faith as a little girl. One evening, he dropped by to put Faith to bed. Kathy said prayers. Flanked by her mother on one side of the bed and her father on the other, Faith suddenly began waving wildly, and her mom, Kathy asked, "What are you doing?"

"I'm waving at the angels! Can't you see them?" Faith asked incredulously.

"No, maybe only you can see them." Kathy replied. At this point, Scott stood to leave the room momentarily.

"Oops, there goes one," Faith grinned as she watched one of the three angels follow her dad out of the room. When Scott returned, Faith excitedly pointed again, "She's back. They are all here again!" With that, Faith resumed her animated waving and Kathy thanked God for the angels that protect their family.

"See that you do not look down on one of these little ones, for I tell you that their angels in heaven always see the face of my Father in heaven." Matthew 18:10

Surfer Angel

Forty-year-old Gail grimaced as her spreading spinal cancer caused a painful bowel obstruction. She suffered excruciating abdominal spasms that convulsed her entire body. In agony, she closed her eyes and prayed, begging God to let her die. She opened her eyes and was surprised to see a young man dressed like a surfer standing at the end of her bed, sadly shaking his head as if saying, "no" or "not right now." She described him with yellowish streaks in a page-boy haircut, parted entirely on one side, which left long hair sweeping across his forehead to the other side of his face. Gail also noticed his blue Hawaiian shirt with bright yellow flowers. Confused, she looked away from the surfer angel for a moment and then looked back toward him, but he had disappeared.

Gail later recounted feeling that her surfer angel was God's way of telling her He wasn't going to be bringing her home yet. It was comforting to know that the Lord heard her prayers even though she didn't get the answer she was seeking. Gail found this answer difficult to accept, because of her extreme physical pain.

Gail asked her husband to call a couple from their church, Jean and Bob, who had prayed with her previously, to see if they had time to come and pray again soon. When they arrived that evening, Gail gasped as her prayer partners entered the room. Jean carried a teddy bear she'd brought to comfort Gail. But it wasn't just *any* teddy bear. This bear stood atop a surfboard, wearing the exact same blue Hawaiian shirt with bright yellow flowers that Gail's surfer angel wore earlier! Gail instantly knew she was not alone and that every detail of her life mattered to God.

"Remember, I am with you always, to the end of the age." Matthew 28:20

Angels Everywhere

I couldn't have foreseen the story I was entering, as I sauntered down the hall, trying to decide which hospice room to play in first. The praise music coming from room drew me. As I peeked in the room I noticed two young men who appeared to be in their thirties. As one of the sons sat with tears streaming down his face, their mother lay unresponsive and dying in the hospital bed. My heart swelled with empathy and I cleared my throat quietly, "My name is Karin Gunderson. I'm a harpist with hospice. Would you like me to play some praise music for you?" He instantly perked up and invited me in, introducing himself as Luke. His brother excused himself to return to work. I played and sang, and Luke's tears flowed freely as the Holy Spirit filled the room with a holy presence.

After I finished playing we began talking about how well-prepared people are before the Lord takes them. Luke told me his father had died unexpectedly about 10 years earlier at the young age of 49. He said that shortly after his Dad died, his mother crumbled under the stress, suffering a nervous breakdown. They lost everything, even their home, and became homeless for a short time. Finally, they secured a tiny efficiency apartment. When they got into the apartment, he and his mother and brother sat side by side on their used living room couch crying, not knowing how to get past this devastating grief.

His mother happened to look up and said, "I wonder how many angels are in here?!" As Luke peered through his tears, he saw a myriad of angels, over 100 he was sure, flying in and out and around the room. Luke commented to me, "It was as though the doors of heaven opened and I could smell heaven!" I asked what it smelled like, and he could not even begin to describe it. He replied that the smell was neither "flowery" nor "perfumy", simply the most lovely thing he ever smelled. I said, "You are so blessed! You know the scent of Christ!"

Luke told me that as these angels filled the room, his Dad, or possibly an angel that looked like him, came and stood behind him and rubbed his back. He said this touch was like any person rubbing your back, but it comforted him in an extraordinary way. He said he had confided this story to only two other people because people don't believe. He told me the experience helped him and his brother and mother make it through the most trying time of their lives.

"The Lord gives strength to his people; the Lord blesses his people with peace." Psalm 29:11

Angels in Lab Coats

Weeping freely through most of the songs I played, Ann held onto a comforting experience of which I was not aware…yet. She told me she and her husband Jack dearly loved harp music. As Jack lay in the hospice critical care unit, she remembered his strong, gentle, and healing hands. She reminisced that he would massage her back after a long day at work.

Ann began to share her experience in intensive care following a colectomy. "A doctor and an attending nurse came into my room after surgery. They were both wearing long white lab coats and spoke to me in-depth about what was to come. It seemed they knew the future. To this day, I cannot remember exactly what they told me, but I asked them what would happen to my blind husband, Jack, if I did not recover. After the doctor and the nurse left the room, I remembered something I meant to ask them. I pushed the button for the nurse. When the nurse arrived, I asked the whereabouts of the doctor and the other nurse. According to *this* nurse, the doctor hadn't been in the area all morning. Even more mysterious is that this nurse said she'd been sitting right outside my door all morning and that no doctor or nurse, other than her, had been in the unit at all! The nurse was certain of this as I was one of only two patients in the unit."

Ten days after the surgery, Ann suffered a massive stroke. Although she was told that she would never again be able to walk, talk, drive, or use her right arm, Ann knew she would receive the healing necessary to care for her husband because of her conversation with the mysterious doctor and nurse. All of her capabilities miraculously returned and Ann continued to care for Jack.

Now, as Jack lay dying, Ann reminded him how she had prayed that he would not be left alone. In spite of her grief over Jack's impending death, she knows that God was answering her prayer to be able to care for Jack until the day the Lord brought him home.

"When my time to die comes, an angel will be there to comfort me. He will give me peace and joy even at that most critical hour, and usher me into the presence of God, and I will dwell with the Lord forever. Thank God for the ministry of His blessed angels." Billy Graham

Blessed and Balanced

In the Pediatric Intensive Care Unit of a Minneapolis children's hospital, the mother of two-year-old Grace, a transplant patient, tenderly rocked her daughter, awaiting her certain death. Across the hall, seventeen-year-old Aaron, also a transplant patient, was reacting to his medication with extreme agitation and combativeness. The nurses paced back and forth, one biting her lip, another wringing her hands. Feeling desperate, they were out of ideas on how to calm Aaron. The hospital chaplain rotated between the two rooms every few minutes. As Aaron's combativeness reached an uncontrollable intensity, the chaplain was again summoned to Aaron's room.

He sat next to Aaron, feeling as helpless as the nurses. His only weapon was prayer. As the chaplain prayed silently, Aaron suddenly exclaimed, "Look! Can you see her?" Instantly, complete peace descended upon Aaron and the tension in his muscles relaxed. All signs of agitation disappeared.

A nurse came into the room and whispered to the chaplain that little Grace had just died. "I know," responded the chaplain softly. "Aaron just saw the angel come and carry Grace to heaven. Look how his whole demeanor has changed."

It was true! Aaron was now completely at peace—his body, mind and spirit blessed and balanced by his encounter with the angel who came to bring Grace home.

> *"Every redeemed one will understand the ministry of angels in their life; the angel who was their guardian from their earliest moment; the angel who watched their steps and covered their head in the day of peril; the angel who was with them in the valley of the shadow of death, who marked their resting place, who was the first to greet them in the resurrection morning. What will it be to converse with them, and to learn the history of divine interposition in the individual life, of heavenly cooperation in every work for humanity!" - E. G. White*

Time to Shape Up

"Serving in the military, my friend, Mike, was a really crazy guy and a heavy drinker. During practice exercises the soldiers were instructed to stay down and move, but Mike came up too high, and a bullet grazed the top of his head. He was unconscious for over 24 hours, but when he awoke, he said there were angels dancing all over the room, especially near the ceiling. My guess is that these were the soldiers' guardian angels, watching over their recovery.

"One angel stopped dancing, looked at him and shook his index finger at Mike, communicating without words that it was time for Mike to shape up." Gary grinned and continued, "After that, Mike never took another drink again! I guess he figured he'd been given fair warning and it was time to shape up!"

"When I was a child, I spoke like a child, I thought like a child, I reasoned like a child; when I became an adult, I put an end to childish ways. For now we see in a mirror dimly, but then we will see face to face. Now I know only in part; then I will know fully, even as I have been fully known."
1 Corinthians 13:11-12

Conclusions

What can we learn from these experiences with angels?

1. We are surrounded by angels, watching and guarding each of us on our path toward home, so we are never alone.

    "The angel of the Lord encamps around those who fear Him, and delivers them." Psalm 34:7

2. Angels will be there for our transition from this life to the next.

    "The poor man died and was carried away by the angels to be with Abraham." Luke 16.22

3. We can trust that we are so loved that angels will dance to welcome us home!

    "Let them praise His name with dancing, making melody to Him with tambourine and lyre." Psalm 149:3

4. We can act in ways similar to angels, whose lives and actions glorify God as they praise God, guide people, provide for physical needs, protect, deliver from danger, strengthen, encourage, and serve as messengers of God's Good News.

    "Then I saw another angel flying in mid-heaven, with eternal Good News to proclaim to those who live on the earth—to every nation and tribe and language and people." Revelation 14:6

5. We are loved, and our loving God has assigned us an angel to be with us and interceding for us.

    "Take care that you do not despise one of these little ones; for, I tell you, in heaven their angels continually see the face of my Father in heaven." Matthew 18:10

How can this knowledge change your life?

1. You don't need to fear. Know that you are surrounded by angels, watching you and guarding you on your path toward home.

    "He will command his angels concerning you, to protect you..."
    Luke 15:10

2. Knowing you have a guardian angel can take away anxiety about the dying process and give you freedom to live more fully now.

    "I am going to send an angel in front of you, to guard you on the way and to bring you to the place that I have prepared." Exodus 23:20

    "Then an angel from heaven appeared to him and gave him strength."
    John 20:12

3. As you follow God's leading, you can bless people just as angels bless your life in unseen ways.

    "Are not all angels spirits in the divine service, sent to serve for the sake of those who are to inherit salvation?" Hebrews 1:14

4. You can accept freedom to live more fully—with abandon—knowing that angels will be there for you now and in your transition from this life to the next.

    "And he will send out his angels with a loud trumpet call, and they will gather his elect from the four winds, from one end of heaven to the other." Matthew 24:31

5. You can look forward to the day when God will bring you home, knowing that your arrival in heaven will be celebrated and angels will dance to welcome you home!

    "...I say to you that there will be joy like this in the presence of the angels of God over one sinner who returns home." Luke 15:10

    "Then I looked, and I heard the voice of many angels surrounding the throne and the living creatures and the elders; they numbered myriads of myriads and thousands of thousands, singing with full voice..." Revelation 5: 11-12a

Ideas for Practical Application

1. You can act in ways similar to angels, whose purpose is to glorify God through their every action. As you follow God's leading, you can bless others just as angels bless your life in unseen ways.

    You can protect and guard the dignity and lives of others:
    - By being an advocate in your area of expertise
    - By the way you vote
    - By the way you spend your money
    - Through volunteering
    - By watching out for the welfare of children in your area or in your extended family
    - By caring for the elderly in your family or community

    An angel came and protected the life of Hagar and her cast-off child because she cried out.

    "When the water in the skin was gone, she cast the child under one of the bushes. Then she went and sat down opposite him a good way off, about the distance of a bowshot; for she said, 'Do not let me look on the death of the child.' And as she sat opposite him, she lifted up her voice and wept. And God heard the voice of the boy; and the angel of God called to Hagar from heaven, and said to her, 'What troubles you, Hagar? Do not be afraid; for God has heard the voice of the boy where he is. Come, lift up the boy and hold him fast with your hand, for I will make a great nation of him.' Then God opened her eyes, and she saw a well of water. She went, and filled the skin with water, and gave the boy a drink." Genesis 21: 15-19

2. You can bring a message of encouragement:

    - To a family member
    - To someone who is ill
    - To someone struggling with grief or depression

- To someone you pass in the grocery store
- To someone in your congregation (look for people who are working hard and give them a pat on the back!)
- To a neighbor
- To anyone the Lord places in your path!

An angel encouraged Paul, who went on to encourage the crew of the ship he was sailing on:

"Last night there stood by me an angel of the God to whom I belong and whom I worship, and he said, 'Do not be afraid, Paul; you must stand before the emperor; and indeed, God has granted safety to all those who are sailing with you.' So keep up your courage, men, for I have faith in God that it will be exactly as I have been told." Acts 27:23-26a

3. You can help calm fears:

- By sharing Scripture and prayer with friends and neighbors.
- By working with children in a church nursery, a daycare, or as a hospital volunteer.
- By emotionally supporting someone who is newly widowed.
- By volunteering in a hospice, nursing home or hospital and sharing some favorite Bible verses of encouragement, like Philippians 4:4-9 (perhaps memorized):

"Rejoice in the Lord always; again I will say, Rejoice. Let your gentleness be known to everyone. The Lord is near. Do not worry about anything, but in everything by prayer and supplication with thanksgiving let your requests be made known to God. And the peace of God, which surpasses all understanding, will guard your hearts and your minds in Christ Jesus. Finally, beloved, whatever is true, whatever is honorable, whatever is just, whatever is pure, whatever is pleasing, whatever is commendable, if there is any excellence and if there is anything worthy of praise, think about these things." Philippians 4:4-9

"Look at the birds of the air; they neither sow nor reap nor gather into barns, and yet your heavenly Father feeds them. Are you not of more value than they? And can any of you by worrying add a single hour to your span of life?" Matthew 6:26-27

If you feel God is calling you to be of service to others, consider becoming a Stephen's Minister, or having similar volunteer training for a caring ministry.

4. You can confer a blessing, like:

    ▪ "God bless you."
    ▪ "I love you."
    ▪ "I'll be praying for you."
    ▪ "I'll keep praying for you." (for whatever their concern is)
    ▪ "Keep up the good work."
    ▪ "I'm blessed to have you as a friend."
    ▪ "I'm blessed to have you as…my daughter, sister, husband, (whatever relationship), etc."
    ▪ "I really respect your integrity."
    ▪ "I'm proud of you."

One simple line can bless people beyond words and can literally change their attitude, their self-esteem, or their lives!

"Do not neglect to show hospitality to strangers, for by doing that, some have entertained angels without knowing it." Hebrews 13.2

5. You can tell someone the Good News of Jesus' love for them.

"Then I saw another angel flying in mid-heaven, with an eternal gospel to proclaim to those who live on the earth—to every nation and tribe and language and people." Revelation 14:6

Devotional Thought

In my experience, angels are seen most often by those closest to heaven—the very young and those drawing near to their heavenly home, either through danger or death. They often report that the angels are dancing! Isn't it wonderful that such a celebration takes place when we come home to our Lord?! It's just like the story of the Prodigal Son; the father rejoices so greatly at his son's homecoming that he immediately throws a big party to welcome him home.

Then Jesus said, 'There was a man who had two sons. The younger of them said to his father, "Father, give me the share of the property that will belong to me." So he divided his property between them. A few days later the younger son gathered all he had and traveled to a distant country, and there he squandered his property in dissolute living. When he had spent everything, a severe famine took place throughout that country, and he began to be in need

So he went and hired himself out to one of the citizens of that country, who sent him to his fields to feed the pigs. He would gladly have filled himself with the pods that the pigs were eating; and no one gave him anything. But when he came to himself he said, "How many of my father's hired hands have bread enough and to spare, but here I am dying of hunger! I will get up and go to my father, and I will say to him, 'Father, I have sinned against heaven and before you; I am no longer worthy to be called your son; treat me like one of your hired hands.'

So he set off and went to his father. But while he was still far off, his father saw him and was filled with compassion; he ran and put his arms around him and kissed him. Then the son said to him, "Father, I have sinned against heaven and before you; I am no longer worthy to be called your son." But the father said to his slaves, "Quickly, bring out a robe—the best one—and put it on him; put a ring on his finger and sandals on his feet. And get the fatted calf and kill it, and let us eat and celebrate; for this son of mine was dead and is alive again; he was lost and is found!" And they began to celebrate. Luke 15.11-24

Prayer

Thank you, Lord, for sending your angels to guide us, to provide for our physical needs in dire circumstances, to protect us, deliver us from danger, strengthen us, and encourage us. We ask that you would help us be like your angels in assisting others as you have helped us.

In Jesus name we pray, Amen.

Chapter Seven
Glimpses of Heaven

Those who are lifted out of this world and blessed with a foretaste of heaven universally report a feeling of complete freedom and peace. Often, they receive the opportunity to choose whether or not to return to their body. Returning to life here seems a sacrifice to most, and is usually only accepted by mothers with young children, or those who know their families would be devastated without them.

Taking It All In

"She's coding!" the obstetrician cried. Helen's heart stopped as she gave birth. She found herself in her favorite pastoral place, a beautiful rolling meadow. "I was so excited with the bright, emerald green of the grass, and the brilliant flowers, that I ran as fast as I could across the meadow, wanting to take it all in. I never got tired and wasn't even breathing hard. I felt like I could run forever!"

When I asked her how it felt to be in this meadow, Helen responded with enthusiasm, "Oh it was better than anything you could imagine! I felt so light and peaceful and happy, like I had no cares."

"How lovely is your dwelling place, O Lord Almighty! My soul yearns, even faints for the courts of the Lord; my heart and my flesh cry out for the living God. Even the sparrow has found a home and the swallow a nest for her young— a place near your altar, O Lord Almighty, my King and my God. Blessed are those who dwell in your house; they are ever praising you." Psalm 84:1-4

Floating in the Heavens

I sat spellbound—completely enthralled—as Joe, a staid German farmer from Iowa told me his story. Respiratory distress had landed him in our critical-care hospice unit where he could receive the help he needed in the few days preceding his death. He asked that I play and sing hymns. "What a Friend We Have in Jesus" opened his guarded heart, and he began to share with me. He related the joy of travel adventures with his beloved wife and the agony of watching her die the previous year. Then he told me of his heavenly encounter.

"Shortly after my wife's death I underwent emergency surgery. My daughter, Becky, brought me to her home to recuperate when they released me from the hospital. Later, she told me that I was really *not* my normal self that day. When I was able to speak about my experience, she began to understand the day."

With tears glistening in his eyes, a quiver in his voice, and a sense of great awe that often forced him to pause for the right words to describe his experience, Joe told me of the mystery he shared with his daughter that day.

"When she brought me home, I came out of my body and I was floating in the heavens—flying between the clouds and gently touching down on them. Soft, beautiful, glowing, pastel lights surrounded me and I knew that I was not alone, even though I didn't see anyone else. Complete peacefulness—unlike anything in this world—filled my soul. I was completely free, with a sense of freedom I never dreamed possible." Forced to stop and clear his throat as tears streamed down his face, Joe continued, "I'm not afraid to die now. I'm actually looking forward to it."

After he regained his composure, Joe continued telling me about the evening he spent at Becky's home. When he came to himself, Becky revealed to him that he had been speaking in tongues all afternoon, a completely new experience for this conservative farmer from Iowa. It was something he had never done before and has never done since. This heavenly encounter prepared him for his journey to heaven. As

Joe lay in a hospice unit, he could hardly wait for his ultimate travel adventure—the day when he will enjoy that total freedom again; the day he will be reunited with his wife; the day the Lord brings him home.

> *"... anyone who speaks in a tongue does not speak to men but to God... he utters mysteries with his spirit." 1 Corinthians 14:2*

The Dress

One of the most awesome, detailed heavenly encounters that I have heard was shared by Lisa. Because she knew her story needed to be shared, I volunteered to record it, and I share it with you here.

I lived in an upscale community as a child with an abusive mother. She forced me to wear outdated hand-me-downs from my cousins who lived on a farm in Arkansas. At school the kids teased me mercilessly. When I refused to wear the dull, brown, gunny-sack-type dresses that buttoned down the front, my mother beat me and refused to let me leave the house until I put one on.

By age twelve I was seriously contemplating suicide. That summer I attended a Bible Camp. During chapel, the minister said to the children in attendance, 'Do you want a friend?'

'Well, yeah!' I thought, skeptical that anyone would *ever* want to be *my* friend.

'All you have to do is ask Jesus to come into your heart,' he continued.

'Okay, that sounds easy,' I mused. 'Jesus, come into my heart.'

Suddenly, I heard nails ripping out of the ceiling and watched as the peaked roof of the chapel opened up to stand straight on top of the outer walls. A sparkly light shimmered and hovered above the chapel. Then I peered down and saw my heart, barricaded by a heavy, dark, ugly door, covered in thick chains with locks and bolts everywhere. It reminded me of Marley in the story "A Christmas Carol." I was shocked to see the amount of chain links I had forged as a naïve twelve-year-old girl just trying to protect my battered self.

Next, I watched as the door covering my heart began to bulge and swell. Then the door burst open with splinters flying everywhere. Chains shattered and fell to my feet. I felt naked and exposed, but before I could think about it, the shimmering light shot into my heart from above. I fell backwards from the power. Vaguely conscious that the other kids around me were uncomfortable with what was happening to me and were moving away from me, I allowed the process to continue.

In amazing ecstasy, I rested, floating in this Love that enveloped me. Finally, returning to my physical surroundings, the roof once again appeared solid and immovable. The other children sat restlessly listening to the pastor as though nothing had happened. For the first time the thought occurred to me, 'He must have come *just for me*!'

This was a small beginning to a life of dependence on Christ and an incredibly close relationship with him, but things still hadn't improved at home. Many times I retreated to a corner to cry. My grandma, who I called Nanny, remained my one earthly solace. Though Nanny lived far away in Australia, I wrote to her about all my feelings, fears and sadness. Nanny encouraged me through her letters.

I married young and soon became the mother of two small children. One day my mother called to report that Nanny was not recovering well from knee surgery. Mom planned to fly to be with her mother, my Nanny. I said I would really like to go with her. She encouraged me, saying my youngest son could fly free with me, and my husband could take care of our kindergartner. My husband refused permission, citing the lack of child care help during his afternoon work hours and the prohibitive expense of the trip.

Mother flew alone to see Nanny and stayed with her and my grandpa in Australia. One afternoon she went to the drugstore to pick up a prescription. To her horror, when she returned, an ambulance stood in front of the house. The EMTs were carrying out my Nanny in only her slip. Mom grabbed one of Nanny's favorite dresses for her to wear when she was released from the hospital. But Nanny was pronounced dead when she arrived at the hospital. Mom asked that she be clothed in the dress she'd brought from home before being cremated.

When the phone rang at 2:30 a.m., I heard Mom sobbing as she told me of Nanny's death. I felt sick to my stomach—like I was drowning in the emotions of not getting to say goodbye to Nanny. I felt angry at my husband for not letting me go and at God for not providing a way. My sadness at the loss of my one supportive family member seemed to overwhelm me. I sobbed for two hours, devastated, until my husband pleaded that he needed to get some sleep since he had to get up at 6:30 a.m. I agreed I would try to sleep, but I kept wishing I could've said goodbye to Nanny and asking God why I hadn't been allowed to see her one last time. Before I fell asleep I asked for forgiveness. 'Oh Lord, I'm so sorry. Please forgive me for these bad thoughts. Forgive me for being angry with my husband. Forgive me for being angry with You. And even though I only got to see my Nanny four times in my life, I accept your taking her, but I sure wish I could've said goodbye to her."

The next thing I knew, two angels with long, brown, curly hair pulled me out of my body and we flew straight up, through the ceiling of my house and into outer space like a shooting star. I watched my house disappear and within seconds earth was just a pinpoint. As we shot past planets and stars, I turned to the angel on the right and asked, 'Where are we going?' The angel looked back at me silently, then looked up and raised her right arm to indicate *up*. Since this angel didn't speak, I turned to the other angel, who appeared identical to the first, and received the same response. By now, I figured no one was going to speak to me so I just stared in awe at the beauty of the universe that enveloped me. I watched a comet streak across the sky and saw its tail burn within a few miles of me. I was speeding past planets and comets and I wondered where I was. 'Hmmm, I wonder what galaxy I'm seeing now?'

Suddenly, I clearly heard a deep voice state matter-of-factly, 'That's the Milky Way, Lisa.'

I was shocked! He knew my name! He heard my unspoken question! I was afraid to ask any more questions.

After approximately 20 minutes we approached a ledge of clouds in the shape of a large tongue. We came from below the cloud ledge and lightly descended on to it. On the ledge the colors were intensely bright, iridescent, pearlescent—purple, blue, green, orange, yellow and pink, like the color of a bubble or an opal, but brighter than anything on earth. I saw huge, carved, pearl gates in the shape of the Ten Commandment tablets, and a man standing behind a podium, with wings so long that they disappeared into the cloud on which he stood. He had charge over the Book of Life, which was open to the middle. The pages on each side of the book stood over 12 inches high. The angel held a long, billowing, feathered quill pen, and busily pored over the book. The pearl door on the right stood slightly open, with an 8-10 foot angel guarding the entrance as if waiting for someone. Behind the gate were 13-15 chubby baby angels, all different sizes, from tinier than a baby to the size of a five or six-year-old. Their skin tones varied from white to black. They were flying, flitting and playing musical instruments behind the gate. Each of the little winged angels was playing a unique instrument: a tiny harp, a tambourine, a little horn, finger cymbals, flute, lute, large cymbals, joyfully making a cacophony of musical noise. I said to myself, 'So this is the welcoming party to heaven!' I burst into a grin, giggling uncontrollably at their joyful abandon.

Inside the gate I saw little children bouncing a ball, a young girl skipping by jumping rope, and small groups of adults standing around and talking. All of them were dressed in white, gauzy clothing.

I thought to myself, 'I should look for the streets of gold.' I had always hoped to see them. Disappointment set in as I saw the streets seemed to be glass, not gold, reflecting the people and angels standing near or on them. It wasn't until later that a pastor told me that, according to the Bible, the gold of the streets of heaven is so pure that it looks like glass.

At the end of the long street sat a giant, flat-roofed town with the tallest building in the middle, and then lower and lower flat roofs, like a terraced city. Years later, I saw a large poster of Jerusalem in a pastor's office and I felt the color drain from my face. I knew that city—I had seen it in heaven!

Now, in my peripheral vision I suddenly glimpsed my Nanny flying to the middle of the cloud ledge on which I was perched. Two angels flew in "V" formation behind her. Nanny's accompanying angels made sure she had a safe landing and then turned and flew away. Nanny immediately called me, "Lisaleine, come here." I wanted to run but the angels held me fast. Nanny's outfit puzzled me. She wore an ugly, translucent, navy-blue, polyester dress with giant, colorful birds of paradise printed on it; her slip was visible through it. As I wished to go to Nanny, the angels released me and stood like centurions on duty. At this point I broke into a run to my precious Nanny! I wondered if my arms would go right through her, but they didn't! I was able to hug my grandma. "Oh Nanny I can't believe that God arranged for us to see each other again so we could say goodbye."

Nanny agreed. 'It's *so* wonderful that God arranged all of this so I could see you. You are doing *such* a wonderful job with your children. Give them a hug and kiss them for me, and tell your husband I'm proud of him, too. But right now, your mother is on her knees on my floor, sobbing in the living room of my house. I walked around her and tried to get her attention, but she wouldn't listen to me. Do you think you could give her a message from me?'

'Sure Nanny, I'll try. What is it?' I answered tentatively.

She looked at me very serenely and said, 'Just tell her God called me and I had to go.'

'Oh sure, I can give her that message,' I agreed, thinking, *that's easy*.

Nanny hugged me and kissed me one last time and said, 'Well, I have to check in now.' Then she walked up to the book and thanked the angel, who handed her the quill pen. He showed her where to sign, she signed and handed the pen back with a nod. The keeper of the Book of Life motioned Nanny toward the tall angel blocking the gate. The angel opened the gate wider for Nanny to enter. As he took her hand to escort her in, she paused, turned back to me and said, 'Lisa, when it's your turn and God brings you to heaven, I'm going to be waiting for you right here behind this gate.'

'Okay Nanny.' I answered. With that, she blew me a kiss, turned and entered to exchange her gaudy dress for one of the beautiful flowing white robes the residents of heaven were wearing.

The gate clicked shut, and I felt the angels once again secure me under my arms. I watched as my amazing outer space journey was reversed… past planets, stars, comets…now earth in view…my home and then boom, back into my body. I held my eyes tightly shut, afraid of what I would see, and just listened. On hearing my husband's electric shaver, I sat bolt upright.

He rounded the corner and said 'You look like you've seen a ghost!'

I responded, 'I think I have!'

I climbed out of bed to call my mom. I described the events and the odd sight of Nanny in her slip with an ugly, kind of see-through dark-blue polyester dress with birds of paradise printed on it.

'That's the dress I brought to the hospital so she would have something to wear!' Mom responded. Now Mom and I knew this was not just a dream but a real happening! How could I have seen the exact dress my Nanny's body had been cremated in?

Though I still miss my Nanny's encouraging notes, I am filled with joy that my Nanny who had begun to show signs of dementia is now completely and perfectly restored in heaven. Best of all, I know she'll be waiting for me at heaven's gate.

"Then I saw a new heaven and a new earth, for the first heaven and the first earth had passed away, and there was no longer any sea. I saw the Holy City, the new Jerusalem, coming down out of heaven from God, prepared as a bride beautifully dressed for her husband. And I heard a loud voice from the throne saying, 'The dwelling of God is now among people, and He will dwell with them.'"

They will be his people, and God himself will wipe every tear from their eyes. There will be no more death or mourning or crying or pain, for the old order of things has passed away." Revelation 21:1-4

"The twelve gates were twelve pearls; each gate was made of a single pearl. The great street of the city was of pure gold, like transparent glass." Revelation 21:21

"But you have come to Mount Zion, to the heavenly Jerusalem, the city of the living God. You have come to thousands upon thousands of angels in joyful assembly, to the church of the firstborn, whose names are written in heaven." Hebrews 12:22-23

The Missing Goldfish

Forty-year-old Janet lived with her husband on an army base. She was not feeling well one afternoon, and her husband suggested she take a nap. "My breathing and heart stopped when I lay down and my spirit left my body. We didn't have a phone, and I watched my husband go back and forth from the pay phone outside three times before finally calling 9-1-1. My spirit went up through our ten-story apartment building, and I could see everything that was going on in each apartment.

I rose up into the heavens and came to a bright golden river. It had a rainbow bridge over it, but the angel Gabriel, standing about 10 feet tall, would not allow me to pass. Across the river, I could see my loved ones who had gone before me. No one had to speak because we could hear each other's thoughts, so it was a different way of communicating."

Janet continued sharing her experience. Still standing at the river, she talked to a woman named Mrs. Stuart, who had tutored her husband, Rob, as a boy. Janet had never met Mrs. Stuart and thought it was interesting she immediately knew who Mrs. Stuart was. Mrs. Stuart recalled a time when Rob asked what had happened to the goldfish she kept in a little glass bowl on the piano. Mrs. Stuart said Rob was mortified when she revealed that her Siamese cat had eaten the fish.

Janet told me heaven was just like I had described it from the stories people have told me—with the greenest grass, mountains, a lake, and a golden river. As she stood in the heavenly realm taking in the beauty around her, she was told telepathically that this was not her time to go, that she still had a lot of work to do, and she needed to go back. She then came back to her body as paramedics resuscitated her.

Upon awakening, Janet told her husband she had seen him walk back and forth three times from the phone booth, unable to decide whether to call 9-1-1. He said, "You could see that?!"

She said, "Yes," and told him all the things she had seen. He was especially astonished that she had met his childhood tutor and was able to recount the story of the missing goldfish.

Janet had so much fun telling all her neighbors what she had seen them doing in their apartments as she ascended through the apartments on her heavenly journey. Now, Janet is not afraid of dying at all. She knows that beauty, wonder, friends and family await her.

> *"But, as it is written, 'No eye has seen, nor ear has heard, nor has the human heart conceived, what God has prepared for those who love him.'" 1 Corinthians 2:9*

A New Heart

At the moment of her heart attack, Liz immediately passed out and never felt pain. Transported instantly into a beautiful, green, grassy meadow by a lake, she stood before Jesus. As an artist, Liz noticed every detail of the heavenly scene.

"It struck me that every single thing emanated light from within, and there were absolutely no shadows anywhere, not even between blades of grass! All the colors were brighter than *any* colors we have on earth, yet they didn't hurt my eyes at all!"

Upon being resuscitated, Liz learned that half of her heart had died. Her health would remain precarious throughout life. Because of the doctor's incompetence, she ended up in litigation to cover the multitude of ongoing medical expenses. Approximately five months later, the law firm scheduled Liz to fly to Texas for extensive testing with the foremost heart specialist in the country in preparation for the upcoming court case.

The week before she flew to Texas, she and her best friend, Sharon, decided to attend a Christian Women's Conference. In the middle of worship, Liz saw Jesus touch her heart and felt she was being healed. At that exact moment, Sharon gasped, turned to Liz and blurted out, "I heard Him say, 'I will give her a new heart.'"

The following Monday, Liz flew to Texas, returning to Mesa the day after her tests were completed. Within a few days, the cardiologist who had cared for her since the heart attack called and said, "I have some rather startling news. There is no sign you ever had a heart attack! There is no scar tissue. There is no dead tissue. For the last five months, half of your heart has been dead, and dead tissue doesn't regenerate. In my 30-plus years I have never seen anything like this. There is no medical explanation for this. The only explanation is that this was a miraculous event!"

Now Liz chuckles as she says, "Not only did I get to be a witness to doctors in two different states, but to a whole team of lawyers, too!" She continues, "I am not afraid of death at all. Whatever happens, I know the Lord will not give me more than I can bear."

Liz knows she is deeply loved by God!

"For I am convinced that neither death, nor life, nor angels, nor rulers, nor things present, nor things to come, nor powers, nor height, nor depth, nor anything else in all creation, will be able to separate us from the love of God in Christ Jesus our Lord." Romans 8:38-39

Wonders that Await

At 62 years old, Mary had seen many things most of us have just read about in the Bible. My time was limited after I played my harp in the nursing home where Mary lived. She had so many incredible things to share that she crammed in as much as she could in our few minutes together.

Mary's husband had died and she has received the gift of being allowed to visit him. "I've gotten to visit heaven many times. It is just like the Bible talks about! They are preparing a really long banquet table there. I also was able to see the Tree of the Knowledge of Good and Evil, which no one is allowed to touch, and the Tree of Life, which spans a golden river. I've been in the throne room and the throne of God is so incredibly bright, you can hardly look at it without sunglasses. A brilliant rainbow encircles the throne. I was allowed to see all of the apostles and got to be with Noah.

There is no need to talk there. Communication happens silently, kind of telepathically, in a different way than on earth. At one point the angel Gabriel thought I'd seen more than enough and abruptly sent me back to earth."

With an ever-positive attitude, Mary concluded her life-changing information by revealing her purpose in the nursing home at such a young age. "I know why I'm here in this nursing home," she stated with confidence. "I'm here to reassure the dying ones of the wonders that await them in heaven."

"Wow! What a wonderful gift you are to so many people!" I responded. "I think you are right on target, Mary. May God bless you as you continue to do his work until the day you get to go home with Him." I gave Mary a big hug and continued on my way!

"Then the angel showed me the river of the water of life, bright as crystal, flowing from the throne of God and of the Lamb through the middle of the street of the city. On either side of the river is the tree of life with its twelve kinds of fruit, producing its fruit each month; and the leaves of the tree are for the healing of the nations." Revelation 22:1-2

Conclusions

What can we learn from these experiences of heaven?

1. There is a heaven, where we will live joyfully with all things made new and perfect after this life.

   "And the one who was seated on the throne said, 'See, I am making all things new.'" Revelation 21: 5

2. We will not have earthly physical limitations in heaven.

   "We will all be changed, in a moment, in the twinkling of an eye, at the last trumpet. For the trumpet will sound, and the dead will be raised imperishable, and we will be changed. For this perishable body must put on imperishability, and this mortal body must put on immortality." 1 Corinthians 51:1-3

   "And if (we are His) children, then heirs, heirs of God and joint heirs with Christ—if, in fact, we suffer with Him so that we may also be glorified with Him." Romans 8:17.

3. We will not feel burdened with stress, anxiety and fears as we do here. We will feel free!

   "God himself will be with them; He will wipe every tear from their eyes. Death will be no more; mourning and crying and pain will be no more, for the first things have passed away." Revelation 21:3-4

4. Nothing in the universe is unplanned or unforeseen. Every detail of your life matters to God. Every dream seemingly unfulfilled is known to your Creator. There is an eternity to fulfill it.

"In your book were written all the days that were formed for me, when none of them as yet existed." Psalm 39:16

How can these stories change your life?

1. They can offer you God's peace, reminding you that loved ones who have gone before you remain safe and happy with renewed life on the other side.

   "For we know that if the earthly tent we live in is destroyed, we have a building from God, a house not made with hands, eternal in the heavens. For in this tent we groan, longing to be clothed with our heavenly dwelling— if indeed, when we have taken it off we will not be found naked. For while we are still in this tent, we groan under our burden, because we wish not to be unclothed but to be further clothed, so that what is mortal may be swallowed up by life."

   "So we are always confident; even though we know that while we are at home in the body we are away from the Lord—for we walk by faith, not by sight. Yes, we do have confidence, and we would rather be away from the body and at home with the Lord. So whether we are at home or away, we make it our aim to please him." 2 Corinthians 5:1-9

   "...and the peace of God which passes all understanding will guard your hearts and minds as you trust in Christ Jesus." Philippians 4:7

2. These stories can help you keep an eternal perspective, knowing this life is only the beginning, and that something bigger and more wonderful awaits you. The challenging events of this life are of little consequence in the span of eternity.

   "So we do not lose heart. Even though our outer nature is wasting away, our inner nature is being renewed day by day. For this slight momentary affliction is preparing us for an eternal weight of glory beyond all measure, because we look not at what can be seen but at what cannot be seen; for what can be seen is temporary, but what cannot be seen is eternal."2 Corinthians 4:16-18

3. These true stories give assurance that we will be reunited with our loved ones again in a beautiful place of joy and peace.

    "In the resurrection, then, whose wife of the seven will she be? For all of them had married her.'

    "Jesus answered them, 'You are wrong, because you know neither the scriptures nor the power of God. For in the resurrection they neither marry nor are given in marriage, but are like angels in heaven. And as for the resurrection of the dead, have you not read what was said to you by God, 'I am the God of Abraham, the God of Isaac, and the God of Jacob'? He is God not of the dead, but of the living."
    Matthew 22:28-32

4. They can offer you hope for something better—true fulfillment. We can see from Scripture and these stories that we will feel different in heaven than we do here. We won't carry burdens of stress, grief, shame, guilt, pain, insecurity, low self-esteem, exhaustion or fears. Each person who tells me about their heavenly experience talks about joy, fun, laughter, love and peace beyond anything we have ever imagined.

    "He will wipe every tear from their eyes. Death will be no more; mourning and crying and pain will be no more, for the first things have passed away." Revelation 21:4

Devotional Thought

How often do you long for the courts of the Lord? Sometimes it seems easier just to be done with this life and enter the eternity that awaits us—the eternity with no striving, stress, competition, unrealistic expectations; no anger, no violence, no daily litany of crimes, murders and deaths that we call "the news," no loneliness, no depression, no grief, no feelings of guilt, of not being good enough, or of not being enough.

I do long for the courts of the Lord! Yet, the Lord has placed each of us here with a special mission to accomplish in this lifetime—a mission that only we can fulfill. The way we accomplish this mission may change over the years, but the focus is always the same, to grow in love for God and for others.

God has chosen us as His hands of service, His arms to embrace, His feet to bring Good News, His lips to speak words of compassion, love and encouragement. Maybe your work here is simply (or not so simply) to learn to know God. Maybe your call is to pray for this hurting, imperfect world. Perhaps you fulfill your calling in your work. Each day a new piece of our mission may be revealed if you look for it. Something that seems small to me—taking a walk with a grieving friend, or calling on a home-bound person—may be very important to that friend and to God.

"Therefore, since we are surrounded by such a great cloud of witnesses, let us run the race marked out for us. Let us fix our eyes on Jesus the author and perfecter of our faith, who for the joy set before him endured the cross, scorning its shame, and sat down at the right hand of the throne of God. Consider him who endured such opposition from sinful men, so that you will not grow weary and lose heart." Hebrews 12:1-3

"For our light and momentary troubles are achieving for us an eternal glory that far outweighs them all. So we fix our eyes not on what is seen, but on what is unseen. For what is seen is temporary, but what is unseen is eternal." 2 Corinthians 4:17-18

"For My yoke is easy, and My burden is light." Matthew 6:2

Prayer

Dearest Jesus,

Thank you for all you endured for me. When I am longing for the courts of the Lord and wanting to be in my true home, help me remember all you suffered on my behalf. Let me not grow weary or lose heart, knowing this life's trials are only temporary, and an eternal glory awaits me. Help me fix my eyes on You each day and run the race You have marked out for me, with my family in Christ, so my life will glorify You, and others will meet You through my words and actions.

Thank you, Lord, for glimpses of heaven that help us keep an eternal perspective in the midst of the difficulties of this present life. Thank you most of all that You call me by name, and that I don't have to be afraid of anything. I love You and appreciate You, Lord. Amen.

Chapter Eight
Encountering Jesus

I grew up in the Christian church, and hadn't really contemplated what people of other religions believe and experience in the dying process before I began working with hospice. I have to say, even as a Christian, I was really surprised to see that at the point of death, it's Jesus who shows up for people of all religions and no religion—Jews, Christians, Buddhists, Hindi, Muslim, atheist, agnostic. After ten years of playing 20-30 hours a week in hospice and a lot of thought on this subject, I have come to this conclusion: Jesus is often the One that people see at the point of death, because he is the only form of God who lived as a human, died as humans die, and rose again. He is the "first fruit" of what our eternal bodies will be like—the first one to have put on an eternal, imperishable body.

I believe Jesus comes for two reasons.

1. More than any other thing in the New Testament of the Bible, it says, *"Do not be afraid."* God doesn't want us to be afraid so He sends His son, Jesus, who was human like us so He looks like us. His presence is non-threatening and welcoming.
2. Because Jesus gave His life on the cross for our imperfections, we can receive the gift of eternal life. *"Jesus said, 'I am the way, and the truth, and the life. No one comes to the Father except through me.'" John 14:6.* Jesus became the *bridge* between this world and the next, offering a way to heaven for all.

Particularly interesting to me is that when Jesus "shows up" at the point of death for people of every religion or no religion, they all *know* who He is and they *know* He is the way home. I'm sure there are a few people who turn Him down at that point, but I've never seen it. I don't know how you could stand in the presence of Someone who knows all your worst faults but loves you anyway, and Someone who has a better plan for you than you could have ever imagined, and say, "No, I'd rather go to eternal nothingness, isolation, or condemnation." When people see Jesus they know automatically that He loves them and has wonderful things in store for them, so they trust Him.

Messiah Revealed

Chanting in Hebrew as Abraham received a massage in one of our hospice units, this Jewish man continued his life-long spiritual journey with praise to his God. Unexpectedly, Abraham suddenly sat up. There in front of him he saw Jesus. In great joy he realized this was his Messiah. Abraham was baptized two days before he died.

"Then they shall be my people, and I will be their God." Ezekiel 37:23

More Than a Dream

Bob's wife, Ann, suffered from ALS; she was comatose and connected to a myriad of tubes. Bob, exhausted from seeing the serious condition of his beloved, fell asleep one night in the chair next to her bed.

He began dreaming that he saw a huge, dark, open hole. He could see that there were people standing all around this opening. Bob soon recognized all the people as friends and relatives who had previously died. He ventured over to the edge of the chasm and discovered that they were all looking down at Ann. Bob asked what they were waiting for. They said they were waiting for Jesus to come and bring Ann home. Then Bob saw Jesus joyfully calling down to Ann, "Come on up!" Bob suddenly awoke with a start as the sun was creeping in through the hospital-room window. This experience seemed more real than any dream he'd ever had. As the day wore on, the dream faded, as dreams do in the hubbub of the day.

That evening Bob's niece visited them at the hospital and told him that she'd had an astonishing dream the night before. "I dreamt that many people were standing over this large opening in the clouds looking down on Ann. They said they were waiting for Jesus to come and bring Ann home." As she revealed the dream to Bob it was apparent that they'd experienced the same vision—more than just a dream!

"And if I go and prepare a place for you, I will come again and will take you to myself, so that where I am, there you may be also." (Jesus) John 14:3

Mom's Visits

No one was making oatmeal, but each morning the scent of oatmeal was obvious to everyone who entered Stephanie's home. Her mother had made oatmeal every morning, but it had been nearly two years since her Mom's death. As Stephanie's father's health began to deteriorate, she and her husband brought him to live with them. *Could Mom actually be coming here?* Stephanie wondered. She couldn't believe that her deceased mother could be visiting her earthly home, but I reminded her, "The Bible speaks of the great cloud of witnesses that surrounds us."

Stephanie responded, "Yes, that thought crossed my mind as well. One morning my dad told me Mom came to visit him in the night. She said she'd be coming to bring him home soon."

After hearing this, Stephanie was sure that the scent of oatmeal had to be a sign from her mother. The next morning, upon waking to the familiar scent, she spoke aloud to her mother, "Mom, you don't have to worry about Dad. We'll keep him right here with us and I'll take good care of him, so you don't need to worry about him." After that day the scent no longer filled the house in the mornings.

On the day before Stephanie's dad died, he whispered to Stephanie. "Mom came to me again last night. She told me it would not be her that would bring me home. It will be Jesus."

Very early the next morning, Stephanie and her husband, both very sound sleepers, simultaneously sat straight up in bed at 2:00 a.m.

At this point in her story, Stephanie's excitement overflowed, "We felt the presence of the Lord in our home. We ran down the stairs to my Dad's bedroom and he must have just died, because he still had air in his lungs when we turned him over. And I know—without a doubt—that Jesus came to get him, because we felt Jesus' presence in our home, unmistakably!"

"In my Father's house there are many dwelling-places. If it were not so, would I have told you that I go to prepare a place for you? And if I go and prepare a place for you, I will come back and take you to be with Me that you also may be where I am." John 14:2-3

Jesus—the Bright Morning Star

"I was really surprised at how beautiful and peaceful dying was," Frank said. "My dad was dying, and most of the family had gone home for the evening. My sister and I were sitting next to Dad's bed, and his breathing began to slow. He looked completely peaceful, and was not struggling at all for the first time that day. The room was dark, except for a little light on the headboard of his roommate's bed. Suddenly the room filled with the brightness of daylight. The light descended first upon my dad's heart, and then spread to illuminate his entire body. I knew it was Jesus—the Light of the world! As the light receded, my dad peacefully left the room to go to his heavenly home. My sister and I sat silently in awe, feeling privileged to have been there when Dad went home. This encounter with Jesus was very encouraging in and of itself, but even more incredible is that this exact scenario has happened to other people in our family at various times, and has greatly blessed all of us."

" 'It is I, Jesus, who sent my angel to you with this testimony for the churches. I am the root and the descendant of David, the bright morning star.' " Revelation 22:16

"Do not worry about anything, but in everything by prayer and supplication with thanksgiving let your requests be made known to God. And the peace of God, which surpasses all understanding, will guard your hearts and your minds in Christ Jesus." Philippians 4:6-7

Not Too Grumpy for Jesus

Harold, a life-long Minnesota farmer, was one of those "grumpy old men." No one liked to be around him. For years his grown children prayed he would come to know God's love, but Harold didn't want anything to do with *religion.*

Now only days away from dying, he phoned his son, "Can you come over?"

"Sure, Dad," Alan answered, wondering what could be so urgent that his Father would call him away from his work day. "I'll be right there."

As Alan walked into the hospital room he couldn't believe the eager, joyful look on his father's ever-sour, angry-looking face.

"You probably won't believe this, Alan, but I'm going to tell you anyway," Harold burst out with a grin. "I was just lying here in my bed and all of a sudden Jesus was here! He took my hands and said, 'Your sins are forgiven.' What a relief! I feel like a large weight has been lifted from my shoulders. He accepted *me,* with all my faults." Dad paused, then continued quietly, "I know I haven't been very nice."

"I forgive you too, Dad," Alan responded with compassion. "The important thing is that now you know that you are forgiven and accepted."

"Well, that's not all!" Dad exclaimed. "Jesus stayed and talked with me for a couple hours. We laughed and talked, and I just *love* Jesus!"

"Wow! Thank you for sharing that, Dad. I can't tell you how much it means to me after all the years we've prayed you'd come to know Him. God is good!"

"Jesus said..., 'I am the resurrection and the life. Those who believe in me, even though they die, will live, and everyone who lives and believes in me will never die...'" John 11:25-26

An Arm around My Shoulder

A nurse for many years, Sherry treasures an extraordinary memory from one particular day at work. "One time I walked into a room where a patient was near death. She gawked at me, gulped, and asked tentatively, 'Are you an angel?'

'No, I'm a nurse,' I responded, confused by her strange remark.

'Then why does Jesus have his arm around your shoulder?' she continued.

I was momentarily speechless, which doesn't happen very often, then I responded, 'I guess He must think I need Him... and I do!'"

"In a little while the world will no longer see me, but you will see me; because I live, you also will live. On that day you will know that I am in my Father, and you in me, and I in you. They who have my commandments and keep them are those who love me; and those who love me will be loved by my Father, and I will love them and reveal myself to them." John 14:19-21

Jesus Loves the Little Children

Ryan was born with severe disabilities caused by cerebral palsy, and he really began to deteriorate when he turned 11 years old. His parents would often hear Ryan talking in his room and would rush to his side to see if he needed something. When they would arrive in his room and ask if he was calling them, his usual halting response was, "No, I was just talking with Jesus."

I love that! I love that Jesus cares so much for those who have no power or prestige or position in the world; that He comes personally to offer reassurance and companionship as they draw closer to their heavenly home. I'm sure there has never been a god imagined in any other religion that is so personal and caring; no other god that sees worth in a child that has no control of arms or legs and can barely raise his head; no other god who would bother to sit and visit with a boy who struggles to speak each word. Our God is loving and accepting. His actions are noble and beyond our comprehension.

> *"Jesus said to them, 'Let the little children come to me, and do not hinder them, for the kingdom of God belongs to such as these. I tell you the truth, anyone who will not receive the kingdom of God like a little child will never enter it.' And He took the children in His arms, put His hands on them and blessed them." Mark 10:14-16*

Wishing It was My Turn

Admittedly jealous that her husband would reach heaven before her, Nancy grieved her husband's sudden closeness to death since he had never been sick. As I played harp for the couple, I sympathized with Nancy as she talked more about her envy that her husband gets to go and she must stay. She then told me of a near-death experience from 1972. Since then, she had not been afraid of death, but actually looked forward to the day when she would get to go to heaven.

"My heart stopped while I was in the hospital," Nancy told me. "I could see my body down below, surrounded by people frantically working. I didn't know anyone who was there. I hovered in an upper corner of the room, but there wasn't a ceiling above me—only blue sky, clouds, bright lights and flowers in the distance. I saw Jesus' robe flowing down at an angle. Suddenly I saw my Dad running toward me and I heard my mother calling excitedly, 'Come on, Baby!' Mom told me it was beautiful and wonderful there, but when I looked down at my body, there were tears coming from my eyes. None of my loved ones were in the room. I just felt like it wasn't the right time to go, so I went back to my body."

The next morning as I read my devotions, I realized God was confirming to me that Nancy's vision of Jesus' robe was real, as I read, *"In the year that King Uzziah died, I saw the Lord seated on a throne, high and exalted, and the train of his robe filled the temple." Isaiah 6:1*

It Is Well with My Soul

"You're not going to believe what happened!" Rose said as she met me at the door to the hospice unit. For several weeks I had the privilege of playing harp and singing for her mother, a special little southern lady named Betty. Betty *loved* the Lord and she loved hymns. If I had stayed all day, she would've just kept giving me one old-favorite hymn request after another. Since I can't stay more than 15-20 minutes in each room, Rose asked if I could bring them one of my hymn CDs . She wanted her mom to be able to enjoy the music when I wasn't there, so I brought one later that day.

The following week our social worker, whose doorframe is six inches from Betty's, met me at the door. She informed me Rose had the *brilliant* idea of leaving my CD playing just one song in Betty's room for an entire day. The song was Betty's favorite hymn, "It is Well with My Soul." The social worker exclaimed, "I know all the words, but I never want to hear it again!"

As I entered Betty's room, I noticed she had declined quite a bit and wasn't speaking much anymore, but occasionally she would say, "It is well…..It is well with my soul."

The following week when I arrived, Betty's daughter, Rose, rushed out to greet me. She said, "You will never believe what happened. My mom had a massive stroke on Sunday and they told me she wasn't going to wake up anymore. I left instructions for the nurses to play your hymn CD 24 hours a day. Three days later Mom sat straight up in bed sobbing, 'Jesus, don't leave me! Please, don't leave me!' It took us over an hour to get her calmed down, but when we finally did, she told us that when she had the stroke, Jesus came and took her to heaven. *She had seen the place He had prepared for her and even seen her parents!* They looked like they were 25-45 years old, in the prime of life (a commonly reported experience). Mom did not want to come back and was distraught at finding herself back in her dying body. She had been told that it was not quite time yet, but that the angels would be ministering to her in the meantime." Rose continued with her report. "I finally left her room for about 20 minutes to run some errands the next morning. When I came back, I started to open the blinds, but then I noticed my mother was luminescent—glowing and sparkling. I said, 'Mom what happened to you?!!'"

"Mom smiled the happiest smile and said, 'Oh, the angels have been kissin' on me!'

'Why is it all over your arms?' I responded.

'Well, I needed a hug, too!!' she added as though I should have known."

Now, three days after the angel kisses, Rose invited me into the room to see Betty sparkling. It was amazing! Almost every wrinkle had disappeared, and the only indication that she was elderly was her perfectly white hair. Betty only remained here on earth a few more days before God brought her home, but what a witness she left!

"Look to him, and be radiant;" Psalm 34:5a

Taking Jesus' Hand

"My Mom's death was awesome!" Mark responded when I asked him how he was doing. He'd called me to play harp and sing for her funeral. I'd never heard anyone describe their mother's death in this way, so I was pleased when he decided to share his story with me.

When I had played in his mom's hospice room, he had told me he felt his mother was clinging to life, waiting for his sister, Cheryl, to arrive from Saudi Arabia. "When my sister gets here, I know something's going to happen!" Mark said, even though his mother had been unconscious for five days. His mother feared Cheryl didn't know the Lord.

"When we picked up my sister at the airport, we told her we felt Mom was holding on in fear that Cheryl wasn't *saved*. Even though my mom was still unconscious when we arrived, my sister confessed her sin and told Mom that she loves Jesus."

Although Mom had not awakened for several days, she opened her eyes widely at this point. Mark sensed she was seeing angels. She then She then looked at her three children and said, "I love *you*." They began to cry and she said sympathetically, "Awww...., I just want to go home."

"I told her, 'It's okay, Mom. You can take Jesus' hand and go with Him.' With that, she looked toward an upper corner of the room with the most joyful smile on her face. She reached out her hand. Her breathing slowed and we felt her spirit leave the room with Jesus as we watched her grasp His invisible hand."

"The Lord is near to all who call on Him." Psalm 145:18

Lonesome for Jesus

"My mom loves the Lord!" Divina said, trying to paint a portrait of Adoracion that would assist me in choosing music for her mom as she neared death. "She reads her Bible daily. Last Christmas she wrote a card to Jesus, telling Him she was lonely and wanted to come home." Adoracion's family felt torn. They hoped she would live until the rest of the family could join them from the Philippines, but didn't want her to suffer. I played instrumental hymns in the room while Divina and her family went to try to obtain emergency visas for the rest of Adoracion's family.

Sadly, they returned with the news the visas were denied. Resigning themselves with quiet tears, that Adoracion would not see her other daughter, her sister and the rest of her loved ones while on earth, they asked if I knew the Amy Grant song, "El Shaddai." It had been awhile since I'd sung it, but I remembered it, so we sang it together a cappella. During the song, Adoracion opened her eyes to greet her Lord.

Suddenly the phone rang. Adoracion's daughter, Maria, was calling from the Philippines. Maria realized her mother was dying when her living room spontaneously filled with the scent of roses. The family put the phone to Adoracion's ear and Maria said a tearful goodbye from thousands of miles away. Adoracion slipped peacefully away with her Lord Jesus whom she'd longed to join for years, while I prayed with the family. I thanked God for Adoracion's faithful service to Him, asked that the family be guided during this difficult time, and prayed that they would feel their mother's presence and Jesus' loving arms around them at lonely times.

"Blessed are those who mourn, for they will be comforted."
Matthew 5:4

Things to Do

"I have a story to share with you," Millie grinned as she approached me after one of our Heavenly Harp concerts. Then she turned serious. "I almost died. I was very ill and in terrible pain, but the doctors couldn't do anything. Day after day I prayed for Jesus to take me home."

Millie was tiny-- less than five feet tall--but light beamed from her withered face. "One day when I couldn't take the pain anymore, I pleaded with the Lord to bring me to my heavenly home. When I opened my eyes, Jesus was standing in the corner. He smiled so compassionately at me and said, "I'd love to bring you to my home, Millie, but I still have things I need you to do here."

"Since that day," the tiny woman continued, "I've taught confirmation classes to junior high students for 23 years!"

"Wow," I responded, "He really did have something for you to do!"

"Very truly, I tell you, the one who believes in me will also do the works that I do and, in fact, will do greater works than these, because I am going to the Father." John 14:12

The Hidden Cross

It's an odd thing to hear yourself singing as you walk quietly down a hall. It seemed even odder to me, when my Christian Heavenly Harp CD was juxtaposed with the scene inside the hospice room. An Egyptian woman in traditional dress sat solemnly near her 20-year-old granddaughter, Mariah, lying unconscious in a bed of beautifully-colored rose petals with crystals strung across each window. Rainbow flecks shimmered around the room. On the other side of Grandma Adinah sat her daughter, Layla, the mother of the dying Mariah.

I peeked in and said, "That's me singing. Would you like to hear me live?" They welcomed me to Mariah's bedside. I asked if they wanted spiritual music, like on my CD, and they responded affirmatively. I wanted a song that would really envelop them in love, so I chose "Spirit Song" on the spur of the moment. Just before I got to the chorus that says, "Jesus, oh Jesus, come and fill your lambs…," I remembered the social worker telling me this was a family of non-practicing Muslims. Suddenly I realized the chorus was going to be inappropriate, but I didn't want to stop in the middle of the song, so I went ahead and finished it.

Since I'd already sung about Jesus, I decided to share my experience as a hospice harpist. "If I hadn't had a faith when I started, I would by now. Almost everyone sees friends or loved ones who have gone before them, who are sent to answer their questions and help prepare them for what is to come. Often, music seems to open that door and people who are near death start having conversations with people I can't see.

"Many people also see angels, and they are almost always dancing. I love the thought that the angels dance to welcome us home." Wanting them to understand why my faith is in Jesus, I continued: "At the point of death, people go so peacefully it's almost imperceptible, or they may have been in a coma for a week or more and suddenly they sit straight up, extend their arms and say, "I see Jesus," or "Take me home, Jesus." I remember one lady said, "Who's that standing at the end of my bed?... Oh, it's you Jesus!" And then she was gone.

I noticed Layla elbowing Grandma Adinah, who understood English, but spoke very little. They nodded at each other in agreement. Then Layla shared, "My mom has been a Muslim all her life. But a few years ago she had open heart surgery. During the surgery, Jesus appeared in a white robe with hair that appeared blond because of the brilliant glow. He stood to the right of her leg near the operating table. Grandma told me that *He* is the reason she is alive now. Shortly after that experience she asked if I would get her a cross."

With that, Layla turned to Grandma Adinah and lifted a dainty gold chain from inside her kaftan. There was the cross. Adinah nodded and smiled.

Now I know why the family are *non-practicing* Muslims. I left them with my CD of stories, and a prayer that it will be used to help others.

"You have given Him authority over all people, to give eternal life to all whom You have given Him. And this is eternal life that they may know You, the only true God, and Jesus Christ whom You have sent."
John 17:2-3

Making Sure Jesus Stays

One of my favorite moments happened when I was playing for a sweet lady who I figured must have been a teacher. Close to death, all of a sudden, she became uncharacteristically lively. She pointed her finger at an invisible presence next to her bed and said, "Now, Jesus, you just stay right there and don't you move!"

She wanted to make sure she wasn't going to lose Him at that point!

"For where two or three are gathered in my name, I am there among them." Matthew 18:20

I Think It's Jesus

Irvin, an atheist psychologist, did not want to visit with our hospice chaplain. The chaplain said, "We don't have to talk about God. You can just tell me what you're going through."

Irvin felt comfortable with that, so every day for the next couple weeks, the chaplain visited and Irvin told her what he was experiencing. On the day he died, he told the chaplain he saw a river, and there was someone on the other side, beckoning him to cross over.

"Do you know who it is?" she asked curiously.

The atheist, Irvin, nodded and responded, "I think it's Jesus!"

He then went peacefully with Jesus at that very moment.

More than any other time in my hospice work, I was awestruck with the mercy and compassion of God. This atheist might have considered faith to be just an emotional "crutch" for those he counseled as a psychologist. Yet he was invited home by the very God he scorned. Now *that* is grace!

"The Lord is not slow about His promise, as some think of slowness, but is patient with you, not wanting any to perish, but all to come to repentance." 2 Peter 3:9

Conclusions

What can we learn from these encounters with Jesus?

1. We can know Jesus is compassionate; He cares about our sorrows, our stress, our loneliness, our physical needs, and He wants to be the answer to each of these things.

    "Therefore I tell you, do not worry about your life, what you will eat or what you will drink, or about your body, what you will wear. Is not life more than food, and the body more than clothing? Look at the birds of the air; they neither sow nor reap nor gather into barns, and yet your heavenly Father feeds them. Are you not of more value than they? And can any of you by worrying add a single hour to your span of life? And why do you worry about clothing? Consider the lilies of the field, how they grow; they neither toil nor spin, yet I tell you, even Solomon in all his glory was not clothed like one of these. But if God so clothes the grass of the field, which is alive today and tomorrow is thrown into the oven, will he not much more clothe you—you of little faith? For it is the Gentiles who strive for all these things; and indeed your heavenly Father knows that you need all these things. But strive first for the kingdom of God and his righteousness, and all these things will be given to you as well." Matthew 6:25-33

2. We learn that God the Father sent Jesus to be our bridge, offering us a way into a joy-filled, eternal life that begins when we become His.

    "Jesus said to him, 'I am the way, and the truth, and the life. No one comes to the Father except through me." John 14:6

"Blessed be the God and Father of our Lord Jesus Christ, who has blessed us in Christ with every spiritual blessing in the heavenly places just as He chose us in Christ before the foundation of the world to be holy and blameless before Him in love. He destined us for adoption as His children through Jesus Christ, according to the good pleasure of His will, to the praise of His glorious grace that He freely bestowed on us in the Beloved." Ephesians 1:3-6

3. We learn that Jesus is available to help us now.

    "I will do whatever you ask in My name, so that the Father may be glorified in the Son. If in My name you ask for anything, I will do it." John 14: 13-14

    "If you love Me, you will keep My commandments. And I will ask the Father, and He will give you another Counselor, to be with you forever. This is the Spirit of truth, whom the world cannot receive, because it neither sees Him nor knows Him. You know Him, because He abides with you, and He will be in you." John 14:15-17

4. We learn Jesus will come to bring us to His home—our eternal, amazing, perfect home!

    "And this is the will of Him who sent Me, that I should lose nothing of all that He has given Me, but raise it up on the last day. This is indeed the will of my Father, that all who see the Son and believe in Him may have eternal life; and I will raise them up on the last day." John 6:39-40

How can this knowledge change your life?

1. We can relax and not worry about the future.

   "So do not worry about tomorrow, for tomorrow will bring worries of its own. Today's trouble is enough for today." Matthew 6:25-34

   "Do not worry about anything, but in everything by prayer and supplication with thanksgiving let your requests be made known to God. And the peace of God, which surpasses all understanding, will guard your hearts and your minds in Christ Jesus." Philippians 4:6-7

2. We find joy in the knowledge that Jesus Christ is for us. He longs to be our bridge to God and eternal life. He longs to wrap us in His love and bring us home.

   "Everything that the Father gives Me will come to Me, and anyone who comes to Me I will never drive away..." John 6:37

   "He brought me to the banqueting house, and His banner over me was love." Song of Songs 2:4

3. We can rest in the knowledge that it is God's will that we receive a joy-filled, eternal life starting as soon as we accept it.

   *"For God so loved the world that He gave His only Son, so that everyone who believes in Him may not perish but **has** eternal life." John 3:16*

   "But do not ignore this one fact, beloved, that with the Lord one day is like a thousand years, and a thousand years are like one day. The Lord is not slow about his promise, as some think of slowness, but is patient with you, not wanting any to perish, but all to come to repentance." 2 Peter 3:8-9

4. We can look forward with anticipation to Jesus bringing us home to heaven!

    "In my Father's house there are many dwelling-places. If it were not so, would I have told you that I go to prepare a place for you? And if I go and prepare a place for you, I will come again and will take you to myself, so that where I am, there you may be also." John 14:2-3

    "Jesus said to her, 'I am the resurrection and the life. Those who believe in me, even though they die, will live, and everyone who lives and believes in me will never die." John 11:25-26

Ideas for Practical Application

- Because we don't need to worry about the future, we can generously focus on the well-being of others. If we need to ask for help or assistance, we give another person the opportunity to be generous.

  "Do not store up for yourselves treasures on earth, where moth and rust destroy and where thieves break in and steal; but store up for yourselves treasures in heaven, where neither moth nor rust consumes and where thieves do not break in and steal. For where your treasure is, there your heart will be also." Matthew 6:19-21

  "But strive first for the kingdom of God and His righteousness, and all these things will be given to you as well." Matthew 6: 33

- Consider spending some quiet time in the presence of the Lord. Hear Him tell you the things you have longed to hear. What is He saying to you? Here are some of the things I would love to hear.
  - » "Well done good and faithful servant."
  - » "I know your pain."
  - » "You are precious to me."
  - » "I am in control, so lean on Me."
  - » "It's okay to rest in Me when you are tired. You don't need to strive all the time."
  - » "Thank you for being you."
  - » "I'm so pleased with how you use the gifts I give you."

Devotional Thought

When people share stories of seeing departed loved ones, they speak of them being at the peak of health and in the prime of life. The Bible says Jesus is the "first fruit" of those raised to eternal life. I believe this is why He is the One that people see, and not other forms of God. He is the only One who came as a human, who arose from the dead with a new eternal body. We know a little of what our next body will be like as we look at Jesus' appearances to people after his resurrection. We know:

- He doesn't need a door to enter a room.
- He still eats.
- He can appear in places miles apart within a short span of time.
- He told us he will never die again.
- He ascended into heaven.
- He is recognizable when he chooses to be.
- His wounds from this life are still evident.

In God's Word, the Apostle Paul speaks of our heavenly bodies:

"So will it be with the resurrection of the dead. The body that is sown is perishable, it is raised imperishable; it is sown in dishonor, it is raised in glory; it is sown in weakness, it is raised in power; it is sown a natural body, it is raised a spiritual body...So it is written: 'The first man Adam became a living being,' the last Adam (Jesus), a life-giving spirit. The spiritual did not come first, but the natural, and after that the spiritual. The first man was of the dust of the earth, the second Man from heaven...And just as we have borne the likeness of the earthly man, so shall we bear the likeness of the Man from heaven." 1 Corinthians 15 (excerpts)

We can be thankful every time we are reminded of our mortality. Whether it's a sign that our body is not as young as it used to be, or when we have a "close call" while driving, or when we notice others getting older and losing some of their abilities, for then we remember that this life is just a speck in the span of the eternity that awaits us.

Prayer

Dear Lord Jesus,

Thank you for being our bridge to eternal joy. Thank you for reminding us we don't have to worry about anything, because we are much more precious than the birds for which you so ably provide. Thank you for the blessings you have provided us in our time here on earth. Give us eyes to notice them and a heart full of gratitude.

We're so glad it's You who will come to bring us home; this brings us great assurance. Help us use our earthly time well. Guide our actions and lead us in Your best path for us. Use us to plant seeds of love and faith in the lives of others, that they may share in the joy of Your eternal kingdom, through Your Holy Spirit. Draw us into an ever closer relationship with You. Amen.

Chapter Nine
Seeing Recently Departed Loved Ones

My Best Friend's Visit

People often speak of knowing their loved ones are near them after they die. I might have assumed people imagined this because they were looking for signs of their loved one, if one of these experiences hadn't happened to me.

Losing my brother when I was 16 was devastating. Then at age 19, when I learned my best friend from second grade through high school had been killed by a drunk driver while riding her bike, I couldn't believe it. I wasn't coping at all; I walked around in a shocked daze for weeks. I couldn't even get closure by attending her funeral, since she was in Washington and I was in college in Minnesota.

God knew the depths of my grief and mercifully allowed Cindy to visit me. Two weeks after her funeral, she came to me in the night. Her visitation was vivid and real. We talked and laughed for hours reminiscing about our fun times together. She also spoke of her life now in the spiritual realm. When I awoke, I understood that Cindy's body had been killed, but her spirit remained very much alive, and she was happy and at peace. I knew that though I might not see her again until heaven, we would someday be joyfully reunited.

Without that compassionate gift from God, I doubt I could have gone on successfully in college. Thank you, Lord, for one more night of giggles and joy with my best childhood friend.

"Come to me, all you that are weary and are carrying heavy burdens, and I will give you rest." Matthew 11:2

Grandpa and the Angel

It was one of those times the phrase "out of the mouths of babes" should have been given some consideration.

After their father Alfred passed away, his two adult sons numbly prepared for his funeral. The sons didn't seem to have any strong church or spiritual ties, but the eldest son, John, asked if I would play for the funeral at a local church. We began talking, and I told him that God often prepares people before bringing them home, and many of those approaching death see loved ones or angels who are sent to prepare them for this part of their journey. Suddenly, a revelation overtook John. Excitedly he reported the events of the morning.

"My nine-year-old daughter, Katie, was very attached to her Grandpa and was devastated by his death. She cried off and on all day and night for the last two days. This morning, she came skipping into the room and announced that Grandpa and an angel visited her, and that Grandpa Alfred is fine and happy. All her sorrow just disappeared, replaced by great joy and peace. I figured she dreamed this, or imagined it, as a way of dealing with her grief, but after hearing what you are saying, I can hardly wait to tell my wife about Katie's experience!"

> *"Take care that you do not despise one of these little ones; for, I tell you, in heaven their angels continually see the face of my Father."*
> *Matthew 18:10*

Heavenly Agenda

No one realized what an incredibly memorable Christmas Lloyd was about to give them. Lloyd had played professional baseball in his younger years. Now on hospice care in his home, his health had deteriorated quickly during the Christmas season. On Christmas Day, the family took turns sitting at his bedside. His niece Anna, a nurse, called the family to his room when it became apparent his time was growing short. The family squeezed together to be near him.

He gazed out the window and exclaimed, "There are a lot of people in the front yard. Oh, those aren't people. They're angels, and they're coming in *here*!"

At this point, fearing he might be dying, his sons decided to take him to the hospital. Lloyd was six-foot-four-inches tall and weighed over 250 pounds, and the thought of safely transporting him down the stairs of their split-level home concerned everyone. They prayed silently on his behalf. Much to the sons' amazement, the struggle down the stairs came not from trying to hold Lloyd *up,* but from trying to keep his feet on the ground! With his feet hovering inches above the floor, angels, unseen by all but Lloyd, carried him down the stairs, because he was too ill to walk.

Lloyd was placed in the car with his eldest son, Matthew. His other son, Dave, drove in a separate car. Sadly, Lloyd was pronounced dead upon their arrival at the emergency room. Dave had unfortunately driven to the wrong hospital, and was delayed in rejoining the family. When Dave finally arrived, still unaware of his father's death, he rushed in the emergency room entrance and, to the surprise of his family, turned around and stepped back outside. He re-entered the room hesitantly and immediately exited a second time. The family watched incredulously, speechless at the sight of this odd behavior. On his third entrance Dave stopped a couple feet inside the door and stared at the upper corner of the room. He nodded his head, smiled, and after a brief pause, joined the family.

They stared at him expectantly, waiting for Dave to explain his odd behavior. "I was so frustrated with myself for wasting precious time when

I realized I had gone to the wrong hospital. When I came rushing through the emergency door, Dad was standing near the ceiling in his baseball cap and uniform. He looked thirty years younger and completely healthy. I thought I was losing my mind, so I turned around and left. I told myself it was all in my imagination and forced myself to re-enter. Dad was still there in the same place, so I left again. I thought this vision of him would disappear if I could just settle down. The third time, I slowed down and took a deep breath before I entered. Dad smiled at me with a look of under-standing and said, 'I have to go now, Son. The game will be starting soon.' With that he disappeared! I guess we know the first item on Dad's agenda in heaven!"

"Your Father knows what you need before you ask him."
Mattthew 6:8b

Nothing Shall Separate Us from the Love of Christ

Despondent, but surviving because of her strong Christian faith, Carol grieved her husband's choice to end his life with suicide. He had sung weekly in the church's sanctuary choir and no one sensed his silent desperation. The first Sunday after his death, Carol couldn't bring herself to face everyone at church, but within a few weeks, she forced herself to return to her church activities and worship services. One Sunday as she watched the choir sing, she looked to the place where her husband always stood. He was there! He stood tall and smiling in his choir robe, singing boisterously and looking happier than she ever remembered seeing him in his lifetime.

Carol wondered if God gave this vision just to her to relieve her guilt and grief. After the service, other people began to approach her, excitedly telling her they saw her husband enthusiastically singing in the choir with a contagious grin on his face.

Carol feels grateful to God for the gift of this vision so she can rest knowing that her husband has joy with God. The relief of seeing her husband's renewal and happiness in Christ has aided immensely in Carol's grief recovery.

"For you have been my help, and in the shadow of your wings I sing for joy." Psalm 63:7

"I caused the widow's heart to sing for joy." Job 29:13b

Final Blessing

As Myra prepared to move away, she was filled with an ominous feeling that she would never see her mother again. Despite this, she fearfully resigned herself to accompany her newlywed husband on his deployment to South America for a two-year tour of duty. The week after her premonition, they left for South America.

As the end of the two years approached, Myra began to think she must have misinterpreted her foreboding and prepared to return home to reunite with her father and her mother, Helen, who'd remained alive, happy and healthy. A few days before Myra and her husband returned home, Myra's premonition came true when Helen was tragically killed in a car accident.

Myra flew home and after her mother's funeral, she felt led to go to her parent's house while the rest of the family gathered at her sister's home. Myra sought comfort and rest in her father's old recliner. She closed her eyes for a moment. As she opened them, she was astonished to find her mother actually coming toward her from the kitchen. Her mother's face and body appeared as though she were back in her mid-thirties. A glowing brilliance radiated from her waist upwards. Myra's mother approached her and said, "There are a few things I need to share with you before I leave."

Helen proceeded to share very intimate things which were extremely helpful to Myra at this particular time in her life.

As she finished the important message she carried to her daughter, Helen suddenly became adamant, "I don't want you to let your dad pine his life away because very soon he's going to have a whole new life."

Following these last words, Helen placed her hand upon Myra's head as if in a blessing. Myra noticed gratefully that it was a physical touch from her mother. She again closed her eyes under the gentle covering of her mom's hand and re-opened them a moment later, only to find that her mother was gone.

True to her mother's word, within two years Myra's father was happily remarried. Myra remains so thankful for the foreknowledge that aided her in nurturing her father through the process of grief toward integration and renewed life.

"Nothing in all creation is hidden from God's sight." Hebrews 14:3a

The Rip Tide

A rip tide tore apart *and* restored Dan's family. After playing and singing for a patient from California and his family, I shared an interesting conversation with Dan, his adult son. Now in his early thirties, Dan confided that his sister, Carry, drowned when she was nineteen years old while swimming off the coast of Hawaii. Authorities believed she was caught in a rip tide.

After his sister's death, Dan began having very vivid and realistic dreams. A few nights after her burial, Carry came to him in a dream and reassured him, "Tell everyone not to be afraid of dying. It is so joyful and beautiful here!"

When he returned to school, Dan felt drawn to a closer friendship with Mark, whose father drowned the previous year. A few months into the school year, Mark went swimming off the coast of northern California and found himself caught in a rip tide, being dragged toward jagged rocks. The waves crashed against the rocks and he was certain he would be killed. He swam with all his might to break free, but his muscles began to cramp and he started to swallow water and go under. Suddenly an apparition appeared to him and told him to let himself be swept to the rocks because he would not be injured. Knowing he had no other choice, he quit struggling and was pushed to the rocks, miraculously escaping with only a few minor cuts and bruises. Excitedly, Mark reported this incident to Dan, and then asked, "Can I see a picture of your sister?"

Dan pulled Carry's high school graduation picture from his wallet. Mark exclaimed with certainty, "*That* is the person who appeared to me!"

"Your Father in heaven knows what you need before you ask Him."
Matthew 6:8b

The Unexpected Visitor

Matt's father, Burt, continued to decline while on hospice care. When he woke one morning, he told Matt, "I saw DJ."

A little confused by his dad's remark, Matt replied, "Yes, DJ came to visit you last night."

"Not David, DJ!"

"Yes," Matt patiently replied again, "Your brother David visited last night."

"Not my brother, David, I saw DJ. He wants you to tell his dad he is fine and happy."

"You mean my best friend from high school?" Mike asked, even more confused.

"Yes."

"But DJ isn't dead!" Matt retorted.

"Maybe you better call his dad," Burt responded.

Uneasy and concerned for DJ and DJ's father, Matt took courage and stepped out of the room to get their phone number. DJ and his dad, Mike, had moved to Washington shortly after graduation, so Matt had lost touch with them the past couple years.

Mike answered the phone and Matt tentatively began, "Hi Mike, this is Matt. Is DJ okay?"

A long pause ensued before Mike responded, "No, he's not okay Matt. He died in a car accident a couple months ago.

Stunned, Matt could barely speak.

"Well, my Dad is on hospice care here in Phoenix, and this morning he told me that DJ came to him and asked him to tell you he is fine and happy!"

Through a gasp and a stifled sob, Mike replied, "Thank you so much, Matt. You don't know how much that means to me."

"I'm always here if you need to talk or need an extra son." Matt said. "You know I'll probably be losing my dad soon. Maybe DJ knew we would need each other."

"Let's keep in touch," Mike replied as their conversation ended. Both men found consolation in knowing that when the physical body stops, life still continues.

"I consider that the sufferings of this present time are not worth comparing with the glory about to be revealed to us. For the creation waits with eager longing for the revealing of the children of God; for the creation was subjected to futility, not of its own will but by the will of the one who subjected it, in hope that the creation itself will be set free from its bondage to decay and will obtain the freedom of the glory of the children of God. We know that the whole creation has been groaning in labor pains until now; and not only the creation, but we ourselves, who have the first fruits of the Spirit, groan inwardly while we wait for adoption, the redemption of our bodies. For in hope we were saved. Now hope that is seen is not hope. For who hopes for what is seen? But if we hope for what we do not see, we wait for it with patience.

"Likewise the Spirit helps us in our weakness; for we do not know how to pray as we ought, but that very Spirit intercedes with sighs too deep for words. And God, who searches the heart, knows the mind of the Spirit, because the Spirit intercedes for the saints according to the will of God." Romans 8:18-27

In order to lovingly minister to both men, the Holy Spirit interceded on behalf of the father who lost his son, and the son who would soon lose his father! The Holy Spirit asks God for everything we need if we are part of the family of God.

"For if you confess with your lips that Jesus is Lord, and believe in your heart that God raised Him from the dead, you will be saved." Romans 10:9

The Mysterious Door

Reminding her husband of Martha Stewart, Teri loved a good party, but her own funeral party?! Teri passed away at 60 years old. Her distraught husband, Duane, asked if I could play for her funeral, since she loved my harp music as she lay dying. I agreed and arrived early to set up. I could only drag Duane away from his organizational duties long enough to have him verify the placement of the songs in the service. After the memorial service, he relaxed, and I took the opportunity to try to comfort him.

"Are you doing okay?" I asked.

"I'm hanging in there," he replied.

"You'll be surprised at how many ways Teri will show herself to you."

"Oh, she already has!" he confirmed.

"Do you mind if I ask how?"

"My daughter and I were preparing for the funeral reception. We sat in the kitchen making a list of everything we would need: the food, paper plates, cups, napkins, silverware. I slipped across the hall to look for linens and noticed the lower door of a large cupboard was open, so I closed it and continued to the closet. When I returned, the door of the cupboard stood open again. I closed it again and finished the list with my daughter. We decided to go to lunch. As we walked out the front door, I closed the door of the cupboard once more.

When we returned from lunch, the door of the cupboard again hung open. I asked my daughter, 'Did you open this door?'

'No, but I've closed it a couple times,' she replied. I thought there must be something wrong with the latch, so I knelt down, but nothing seemed amiss. I closed the door and we returned to our planning at the kitchen table. When I came across the hallway the next time, the door stood open again! As I knelt to close it one more time I noticed something: inside the cupboard door were all the paper cups, napkins and plates we could ever need for our reception today. I didn't know we had a stash of paper goods, but Teri did, and she was determined to let me know!"

In Psalm 139, King David speaks of how the Lord anticipates all our needs and cares for us completely.

Lord, you have searched me and you know me
You know when I sit and when I rise
You perceive my thoughts from afar
You search out my path and my lying down
and are familiar with all my ways
Even before a word is on my tongue,
You know it completely, O Lord
You hem me in, behind and before, and lay your hand upon me.
Such knowledge is too wonderful for me;
Too lofty for me to attain.
Where can I go from your spirit?
Or where can I flee from your presence?
If I ascend to heaven, you are there,
if I make my bed in the depths, you are there.
If I rise on the wings of the dawn
and settle at the farthest limits of the sea,
even there your hand will guide me,
and your right hand will hold me fast.
If I say, 'Surely the darkness will hide me,
and the light around me become night',
even the darkness is not dark to you; the night will shine like the day,
for darkness is as light to you. Psalm 139

Little Pink Wings

It's never too late to be reunited with someone you love, even if they've already died! Clara felt she never really recovered from the death of her precious two-year-old daughter, Emily. In order to maintain her sanity, she held onto her belief that she would someday see Emily again.

A few months before Clara died, she had several dreams in which she was visited by her departed husband, Curt. Each time, he would tell her he had wanted Emily to accompany him to see her, but she was too busy playing. He told his wife that Emily had little pink wings. Then Curt would disappear and Clara would be frustrated because she couldn't find him. Clara told her son, Bill, "I walked to the west and Curt wasn't there, and I walked all the way back to the east, and he wasn't there. I walked in every direction, and I couldn't find him!"

Clara died a couple months later, and Bill is sure his mom is now not only with her husband, but also with her sweet little daughter, Emily, as she flits about on little pink wings.

> *"I declare to you, my family, that flesh and blood cannot inherit the kingdom of God, nor does the perishable inherit the imperishable.... Death has been swallowed up in victory. 'Where, O death, is your victory? Where, O death is your sting?' The sting of death is sin, and the power of sin is the law. But thanks be to God! He gives us victory through the Lord Jesus Christ." I Corinthians 15:53-55*

Our heavenly bodies will be glorious, powerful and imperishable. We can look forward to a day when we won't have to waste energy worrying about getting the right amount of exercise, watching our calories, or making sure we get enough vitamins. We will have ceaseless energy with perfect health and well-being.

In that day, *"those who wait for the Lord shall renew their strength; they shall mount up with wings like eagles, they shall run and not be weary; they shall walk and not faint." Isaiah 41:30*

Won't that be wonderful?! We can use our time carrying out God's plans for our heavenly life, plans that will give us more joy than we can ever imagine; plans that will glorify God in ways we never dreamed possible.

"Since ancient times no one has heard, and no ear has perceived, and no eye has seen, O God, besides you, what you have prepared for those who wait for you." Isaiah 64:4

Conclusions

What can we learn from the experiences of those who have seen departed loved ones?

1. We can know our loved ones who have died are still alive in a "different dimension"...heaven!

    *"For God so loved the world that he gave his only Son, so that everyone who believes in him may not perish but **has** eternal life." John 3:16*

2. We can be sure we are surrounded by the *"great cloud of witnesses"* spoken of in the New Testament of the Bible (Hebrews 12:1). And this *"great cloud of witnesses"* is there to cheer us on and assist us in our journey here on earth. The cloud of witnesses includes our family members and friends who have gone before us, friends who are yet to come, and guardian angels.

3. These stories remind us once again that this life is only one small part of our eternity.

    "For this slight momentary affliction is preparing us for an eternal weight of glory beyond all measure," 2 Corinthians 4:17

4. These stories show us that every circumstance and our very lives are held in God's hand. Jesus says:

    "Are not five sparrows sold for two pennies? Yet not one of them is forgotten in God's sight. But even the hairs of your head are all counted.

Do not be afraid; you are of more value than many sparrows."
Matthew 10:29-31

"Yet, O Lord, You are our Father; we are the clay, and You are our potter. We are all the work of Your hand." Isaiah 64:8

How can this knowledge change your life?

1. It can help you keep an eternal perspective. Things that seem like huge obstacles and tragedies now will seem small in the span of eternity (or maybe even in a year or two).

    "So we do not lose heart. Even though our outer nature is wasting away..." 2 Corinthians 4:16

2. It can help you dare to trust that God will handle all your concerns.

    "I am the Lord, the God of all the peoples of the world. Is anything too hard for me?" Jeremiah 32:27

3. It can give us assurance that we will be reunited with our loved ones. Our loved ones who have gone before us remain alive and well, waiting to be reunited with us.

    "Therefore, since we are surrounded by so great a cloud of witnesses, let us also lay aside every weight and the sin that clings so closely, and let us run with perseverance the race that is set before us... Therefore, since we are receiving a kingdom that cannot be shaken, let us give thanks, by which we offer to God an acceptable worship with reverence and awe." Hebrews 12:1-2, 28-29a

4. It can offer you hope for something better—true fulfillment of all your potential.

    "Listen, I will tell you a mystery! We will not all die, but we will all be changed, in a moment, in the twinkling of an eye, at the last trumpet. For the trumpet will sound, and the dead will be raised imperishable, and we will be changed. For this perishable body must put on imperishability, and this mortal body must put on immortality." 1 Corinthians. 15:51-53

Ideas for Practical Application

- For now, although you can't have a relationship with your loved one in a physical sense, watch for them to show themselves:
  - » in a familiar scent
  - » as you are drifting off to sleep
  - » as you are waking
  - » in your dreams
  - » in a song
  - » in a feeling

- We don't need to grieve as though we will never again see our loved ones after their death. Feel free to speak of them in the present tense, and speak to them!

- Take a walk or a ride in the car (or sit on the couch) with your loved one who has died. Hold his or her hand and feel the joy of being with that loved one. Notice when you speak to them that often you know exactly how they would respond to you. Hear the conversation in your mind and trust that as you think of them, the Lord in mercy allows a connection.

Devotional Thought

As God's child, every circumstance in your life has been sifted through God's loving hands, so you need not fear anything, because you are a priceless treasure to our Lord. Despite this, even though you may feel prepared and have said your goodbyes to a dying loved one, death still seems shocking. When you face your own death, you may not believe it will actually happen. Because we are eternal beings, perhaps we cannot picture ourselves dying. As the experiences in this chapter have shown, it appears that we don't really die. We just leave our physical body and continue on, never actually losing consciousness, and most likely gaining greater consciousness than we were able to possess in our limited physical brains and bodies.

"For nothing is impossible with God." Luke 1:27

"Our suffering is light and temporary and is producing for us an eternal glory that is greater than anything we can imagine." 2 Corinthians 4:17

Prayer

Thank you, Lord, that we will be changed in the twinkling of an eye into a spirit that is not constrained by death. Thank you that soon we'll be together with everyone we love in a place where we will never again suffer from separation, pain or grief.

Knowing an eternity with You awaits helps us dare to give ourselves fully to Your work here and now, even though at times it seems too much for us. Thank you that You care about every detail of our lives and tell us not to worry. Thank you that You promise to provide all we need. Help us dare to trust You fully. We look forward to the day when our bodies will be glorious, powerful, and imperishable. We love You, Lord.

In Jesus' precious name we pray, Amen.

Epilogue

Playing harp and singing for families of hospice patients for 11 years provided me with many rich and meaningful experiences to share. My prayer is that you have been strengthened in your faith and are now looking forward to heaven with hope and fearless joy.

I grieve with the families who have a hard time saying goodbye (for now) to their loved ones. I grieve even more for those who don't understand or believe they can ever see their loved one again. Often I share some of my stories with them to help them in their journey.

Usually by the time we receive hospice patients in our critical care units, the Lord has already brought them to a point of peace and acceptance, and many are impatient to be brought home to heaven, wondering why they are still here. I remind them that as long as they are here, God can still use them. They might simply visualize their family and friends, or perhaps the entire world, held in a sphere of God's light and love; this is prayer at its simplest, without the effort of saying a word. Sometimes their continued presence teaches a caregiver or loved one the way of service and compassion.

This is why I feel it is important we do not give up on life when we feel we are no longer productive, or when we fear the process we must go through.

"... For now we see in a mirror, dimly, but then we will see face to face. Now I know only in part; then I will know fully, even as I have been fully known." 1 Corinthians 13:12

We don't know all the ways God may still want to use us for His glory in our last days and hours. Let's trust God's plan to take us home at the right time.

The saddest thing to me is patients who don't realize, until they are within days or weeks of death, that they have basically wasted their time on this earth. The most common regrets are:

1. "I spent my time unwisely, pursuing possessions instead of relationships. Now I don't know my own children, after I spent all my time working to give them a better life."

    At this point people realize things, goals, and power don't matter. You can't take your "stuff" with you, and if you are alone on your death bed, you are truly alone. Jesus gives the key to a meaningful life in His answer to the question, "What is the most important commandment?"

    "He answered, 'You shall love the Lord your God with all your heart, and with all your soul, and with all your strength, and with all your mind; and your neighbor as yourself.'"
    Luke 10:27

2. "I don't know God, so now I'm afraid."

    People who haven't developed a relationship with a loving God are fearful as they approach death, rather than looking forward to a joyful family reunion. According to St. Matthew, these fears are well-founded.

    "When the Son of Man comes in His glory, and all the angels with Him, then He will sit on the throne of His glory. All the nations will be gathered before Him, and He will separate people one from another as a shepherd separates the sheep from the goats, and He will put the sheep at His right hand and the goats at the left. Then the king will say to those at his right hand, 'Come, you that are blessed by my Father, inherit the kingdom prepared for you from the foundation of the world; for I was hungry and you

gave me food, I was thirsty and you gave me something to drink, I was a stranger and you welcomed me, I was naked and you gave me clothing, I was sick and you took care of me, I was in prison and you visited me.'

Then the righteous will answer him, 'Lord, when was it that we saw you hungry and gave you food, or thirsty and gave you something to drink? And when was it that we saw you a stranger and welcomed you, or naked and gave you clothing? And when was it that we saw you sick or in prison and visited you?'

*And the king will answer them, 'Truly I tell you, **just as you did it to one of the least of these who are members of my family, you did it to me.'** "*

Then he will say to those at his left hand, 'You that are accursed, depart from Me into the eternal fire prepared for the devil and his angels; for I was hungry and you gave Me no food, I was thirsty and you gave Me nothing to drink, I was a stranger and you did not welcome Me, naked and you did not give Me clothing, sick and in prison and you did not visit me.' Then they also will answer, 'Lord, when was it that we saw you hungry or thirsty or a stranger or naked or sick or in prison, and did not take care of you?'" Matthew 25:31-44

3. "I was busy looking out for myself instead of worrying about how my actions affected others."

   "Then he will answer them, 'Truly I tell you, just as you did not do it to one of the least of these, you did not do it to me.' And these will go away into eternal punishment, but the righteous into eternal life." Matthew 25:45-46

The Good News

The Good news is that you can begin a relationship with the Lord anytime simply by speaking to God. Since God already knows everything and wants us to be honest, you don't have to choose your words carefully, just talk to God. *"The Lord is patient with you, not wanting any to perish, but all to come to repentance."* 2 Peter 3:9

Because we cannot even come to repentance (the desire to turn to a life of selfless love) without God's help, *"God so loved the world that He gave His only Son, so that everyone who believes in Him may not perish but has eternal life." John 3:16*

Paul reminds us in Romans 10:13, *"...everyone who calls on the name of the Lord shall be saved."* It's not too late. God is on our side and wants to bring every one of us home to a place where there is no more pain, grief or death, to a place of eternal joy, peace and happiness.

Perhaps you'd like to pray this simple prayer that Jeremiah prayed approximately 600 years before Jesus was even born.

"Heal me, O Lord, and I shall be healed; save me, and I shall be saved; for You are my praise." Jeremiah 17:14

Prayer

Lord, thank you for wanting to forgive me of my sins. Help me let go of any unforgiveness I have harbored toward others, so that I *can* be forgiven. Thank you for saving me through Jesus' death on the cross. I accept that incredible gift that cost You so much, Jesus. Through the power of your Holy Spirit help me turn my life around to be a blessing with my remaining time here. Let me love as You love—always working for the highest good of all those You place in my path.

Heal me, O Lord, and I shall be healed; save me, and I shall be saved; for You are my praise. I do praise and thank you for choosing me before I was even born, and for showering your incredible mercy and grace on me. I praise You for all the beautiful things You place in my life every day. Give me eyes to see them and a heart full of gratitude.

In Jesus' name I pray. Amen

"You have granted me life and steadfast love, and Your care has preserved my spirit." Job 10:12

Blessing from Karin to You

May God bless you as you go from here.

May you know God's incredible love for you; a love that nothing can *ever* change.

May you feel the comfort and joy of God's guiding Presence in your life.

May you have eyes to see God's beauty and goodness in all circumstances.

May you have ears to hear the voice of the Holy Spirit whisper God's love to you in the soft breeze and bird song, and shout it to you in the wild storms of life.

May you taste God's goodness in the bounty of your table and the sweetness of the Spirit's living water within you.

May God bless you as you journey on from here,
so that you may bless others as you have been blessed.

In Jesus' name, I pray for you. Amen

Sharing This Book

It is my hope you will share this book with others, because I have come to believe that all fears ultimately stem back to the fear of death, whether physical death, death of a dream, a relationship, etc. Therefore when you overcome fear of death, you can truly *live,* because you are not afraid of anything. So please share this Good News to encourage others and enlighten them in a unique way, that what the Bible says, is true! This life is only a speck in the span of the eternity that awaits us. Let's make sure an eternity of fulfillment and joy awaits us.

I truly believe that as we allow ourselves to be open to the movement of the Holy Spirit through the experiences God provided for this book, we will rededicate ourselves to love God and *"love others as Jesus loves us. "* I believe God provided this book not only to help take away fear, but to remind us of what really matters—not physical assets or achievements, but love, pure and simple. Love for God and for each other. As each person who pursues a life of Godly love shares with an ever-widening circle of people, the world slowly becomes a kinder, gentler place.

Of course, the Bible says that wars will not cease and peace will not come until the end of this Age, but in the meantime we are called to do our part—*loving the Lord our God with all our heart, mind, soul and strength; and loving our neighbors as ourselves.*

God bless you in your journey.
In God's love,
Karin

Heavenly Harp Ministry – CDs and DVDs

The ministry of Heavenly Harp was founded in 2004 with the mission of combining the unique healing benefits of harp music with the power of scripture and prayer. Heavenly Harp brings God's peace and assurance into everyday life through **concerts, retreats, seminars, CDs** and **DVDs**. Through God's guidance and provision, Heavenly Harp now has seven CDs and six DVDs, each serving specific purposes.

Quiet Reflections: Instrumental Music to Accompany Life CD
- Created for peace and serenity
- Recommended for massage and relaxation
- Our longest CD at 70 minutes
- Creates a peaceful environment at work or home
- Featuring harp, flute, and Native American flute

Heavenly Harp: Inspirational Songs and Stories CDs
- Inspirational two-CD set with favorite hymns like "Amazing Grace," "In the Garden" and "It is Well with My Soul."
- The set was originally intended to decrease fear of difficult times and fear of facing death, but it is popular with a wide variety of audiences.
- 1st CD contains inspiring stories with music
- 2nd CD contains music without the stories
- Featuring harp, multi-part vocals, flute

Thankful Hearts: Songs of Assurance and Praise CD
- Some of our favorite encouraging and beautiful songs including popular favorites like "What a Wonderful World," "You Raise Me Up," and "Somewhere over the Rainbow," as well as hymn favorites "Just a Closer Walk with Thee" and "How Great Thou Art," and contemporary hymns like "Here I am, Lord" and "I Will Rise"
- Featuring harp, multi-part vocals and flute

In His Arms: Songs & Scripture for Serenity CD

- Excellent for decreasing stress, helping with sleep, or for a time of devotion, this CD contains gentle inspirational songs, with favorites like "On Eagles' Wings" and "Jesus Loves Me" and relaxing instrumental pieces
- Featuring harp, multi-part vocals, flute and wind chimes

Nostalgia: Favorite Songs from the 30's, 40's & 50's CD

- Great for calming frazzled nerves with comforting old favorites.
- Excellent for Alzheimer's and Dementia sufferers
- Includes 16 favorite standards from the Golden Age of popular music like "I Left My Heart in San Francisco," "It Had to Be You," "Smoke Gets in Your Eyes," "Stardust," "Pearly Shells," and "Unchained Melody"
- Featuring harp solos and harp with solo vocals

Pure Joy: Masterpieces for Harp CD

- Virtuosic harp solos for lovers of classical music.
- Classical music has been shown to have many positive health benefits
- Featuring pieces like the Pachelbel "Canon in D"

Christmas Music

Gift of Peace: A Heavenly Harp Christmas CD
- A truly unique and beautiful Christmas gift meant to bring peace into the Christmas season with favorites like "Silent Night," "Ave Maria," "Angels We have Heard on High," "What Child is This?" "It Came Upon the Midnight Clear," "Ukranian Bell Carol/God Rest Ye" and more
- Featuring harp, flute, multi-part vocals, Hand bells & **children's choir**

Christmas Morning DVD
- Perfect to set the mood of the Christmas season, See Yosemite National Park sparkling with snow.
- Featuring Christmas arrangements for orchestra, harp, and children's choir on "Silent Night."

Long Winter Evenings DVD
- Perfect for snuggling or relaxing on those long winter evenings
- Sit by the virtual fireplace and listen to the gentle, crackling sound of the fire, or loop the entire 60-minute DVD as it features beautiful scenery and acoustic instrumental music on the harp, flute, Native American flute and wind chimes.
- Two sections feature Christmas music and one relaxing music.
  - » Cozy and classic fire accompanied by "Silent Night," "It Came Upon a Midnight Clear" and "Angels We Have Heard on High"
  - » Peaceful winter and snow scenes with relaxing music, followed by flickering candles with "Ave Maria" and "What Child is This?"

Heavenly Harp DVDs

Serenity DVD
- Gorgeous nature scenery & many of Karin's favorite Bible passages placed intermittently on the screen.
- Featuring Heavenly Harp's peaceful instrumental music with harp, flute, Native American flute and wind chimes

Light for the Journey DVD
- Scenes of mountains, rivers, forests and ocean with the entire story of the Good News told in Bible verses about light.
- Featuring a combination of instrumental music harp, flute & Native American flute as well as several favorite hymns with vocals

The Promise DVD
- Amazing scenery from CreationScapes with Bible verses intermittently over the scenery
- A combination of instrumental music by Tim Janis with harp and flute music by Heavenly Harp, along with several vocal pieces

Season's Wonders DVD
- Explore the wonders of nature as CreationScapes takes you through all four seasons of the year
- Accompanied by a combination of instrumental music by Tim Janis & harp and flute music by Heavenly Harp, along with several vocal pieces.

Karing Journey Wellness Ministry

Karing Journey was formed with the intention of bringing greater levels of wholeness and wellness to body, mind and spirit through natural means and integrative therapies. Karin Gunderson, its Founder, specializes in integrative therapies including Christian hypnotherapy and Reiki, Thought-Field Therapy, Reflexology, Medical Qi Gong, muscle testing for emotional release, and Music Therapy as a Harp Practitioner. With a Natural Health Educator certification from the oldest natural health institute in the Americas, Hippocrates Health Institute, in West Palm Beach, Florida, Karin loves to share her wealth of natural health information, and offer dietary recommendations for vibrant health. As a chaplain with the International Ministerial Fellowship, her greatest joy is the opportunity to pray with others for their healing.

Karing Journey's Integrative Therapy Resources

Resources for Maintaining Vibrant Health & Avoiding or Improving Degenerative Disease

Introduction to Vibrant Health DVD: Prayer Meditation and Morning Flexibility & Strengthening Exercises
- Features Prayer, a Healing Reflection and Morning Exercises that can be practiced while standing, sitting, or reclining.

Healing Qi Gong for Vibrant Health DVD
- Whether you are fighting a degenerative disease or just want to maintain vibrant health, we strongly recommend this as a regular addition for the stressed and/or aging. This DVD increases your physical energy and sense of wellbeing, and features exercises that can be used by people of all ages while standing, sitting or reclining.

Vibrant Health Practices DVD: Daily Regimen and In-Home Integrative Therapies
- A Health Educator from Hippocrates Health Institute, Karin walks you through the daily regimen she uses for maintaining optimal health and a trim body. Includes:
  - » Vibrant Health Diet
  - » Optimal Health with Juicing
  - » Education on six different integrative therapies to help your body heal itself

Soon to come—two new companion books:

Detoxifying & Supercharging your Environment & Body
- The environmental section is a resource for non-toxic options for your home & workplace. It contains everything from building & furniture options to natural ways to clean anything.

- The body section goes into greater detail than the Vibrant Health Practices DVD and aids your success in living healthier in an unhealthy world.

Detoxifying & Supercharging your Emotions & Spirit
- During Karin's education at Hippocrates, she discovered the necessity of releasing negative emotions that have been stored and of dispelling spiritual misconceptions. Both are key components to recovering physical health. This book offers ideas and exercises as well as other resources for detoxifying and supercharging your emotions and spirit.

Resources for Dealing with Symptoms Using Natural, and Non-Toxic Approaches

Depression Pack
Includes:
- Five unique audio CDs designed to help relieve depression
- 24-page booklet with latest natural Health techniques for depression
- Disc 1: *Gratitude*
- Disc 2: *Christian Reflections for Peace, Confidence and Joy*
- Disc 3: *Affirmations for Confidence and Peace*
- Disc 4: *Short, Morning-time Christian Reflections for Peace, Confidence and Joy*
- Disc 5: *Acupressure for Allowing a Positive Perspective*

Stress Release Series
- Five unique audio CDs and an insert designed to help you release stress and create peace, confidence and joy in your life.
- Disc 1: *Gratitude*
- Disc 2: *Christian Reflections for Peace, Confidence and Joy*
- Disc 3: *Affirmations for Confidence and Peace*
- Disc 4: *Affirmations for Students of All Ages: Important Life Skills*
- Disc 5: *Acupressure for Allowing a Positive Perspective*

Encounters with Heaven — Gift Book & Music CD by Karin Gunderson

Purchase the **"hard-cover, gift version"** of this book with a music CD by Heavenly Harp. Available *only* through www.ChristianHarpMusic.com or www.KaringJourney.com

The hard-cover gift version of *Encounters with Heaven* includes a beautiful CD of Karin's Heavenly Harp vocal and harp music.

Encounters with Heaven **gift book and CD** is the perfect, meaningful gift for:

- friends
- every memorial service
- those facing terminal illness
- the grieving
- nursing homes
- those who are going through difficult times
- those who suffer from stress or anxiety
- church libraries
- pastors and Christian workers
- those who are afraid of death
- widows and widowers
- caregivers
- birthdays
- teenagers
- hospice, hospital and nursing home volunteers & patients
- hospice units
- hospital waiting rooms
- Stephen's Ministers and anyone in a caring ministry

"Karin, I am a psychologist. I lost my dear wife one year, nine months and six days ago. You did more for me in one hour than all my colleagues did in one year, nine months and six days. Thank you."
Dr. T. R. Minneapolis, MN

CPSIA information can be obtained at www.ICGtesting.com
Printed in the USA
BVOW010430150513

320750BV00007B/330/P